NARUTO SHIPPUDEN

THE OFFICIAL COLORING BOOK

VIZ MEDIA

NARUTO SHIPPUDEN

THE OFFICIAL COLORING BOOK

DESIGN Francesca Truman **EDITOR** Amanda Ng

Printed in the U.S.A.

ISBN: 978-1-9747-4093-2
Published by VIZ Media, LLC | P.O. Box 77010 | San Francisco, CA 94107
10 9 8 7 6 5 4 3 2 1
First printing, September 2023

VIZ MEDIA
viz.com

SHONEN JUMP

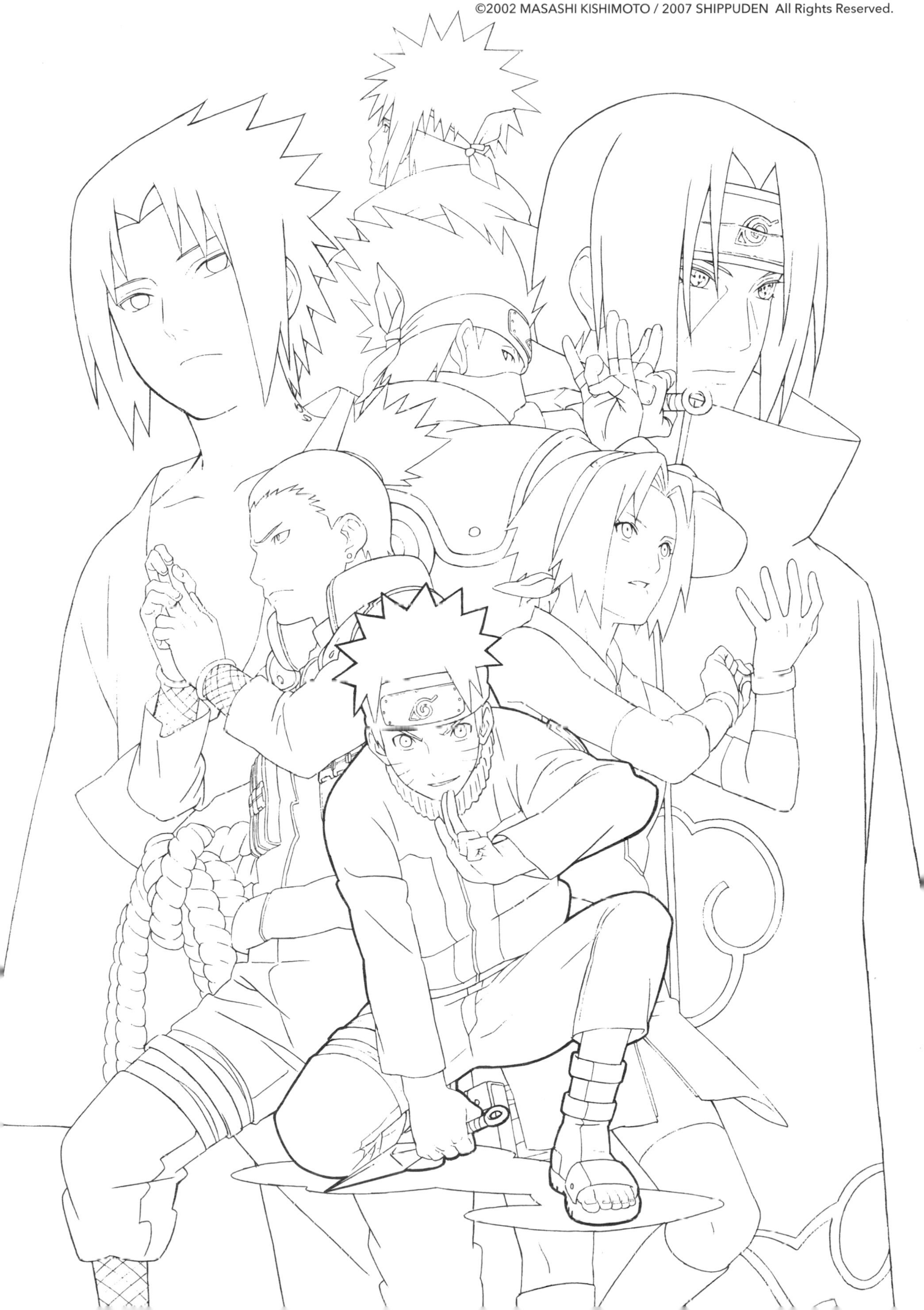

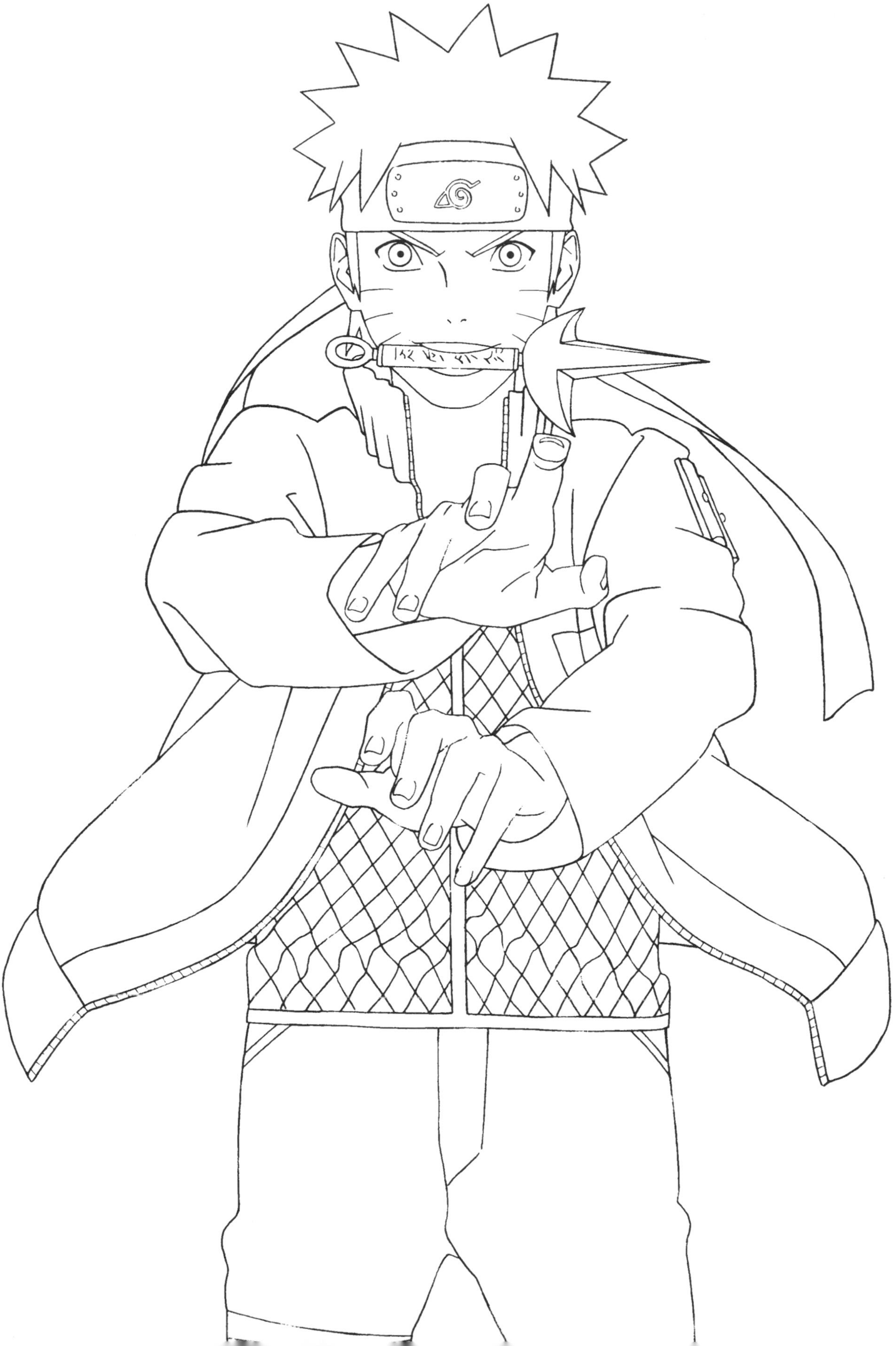

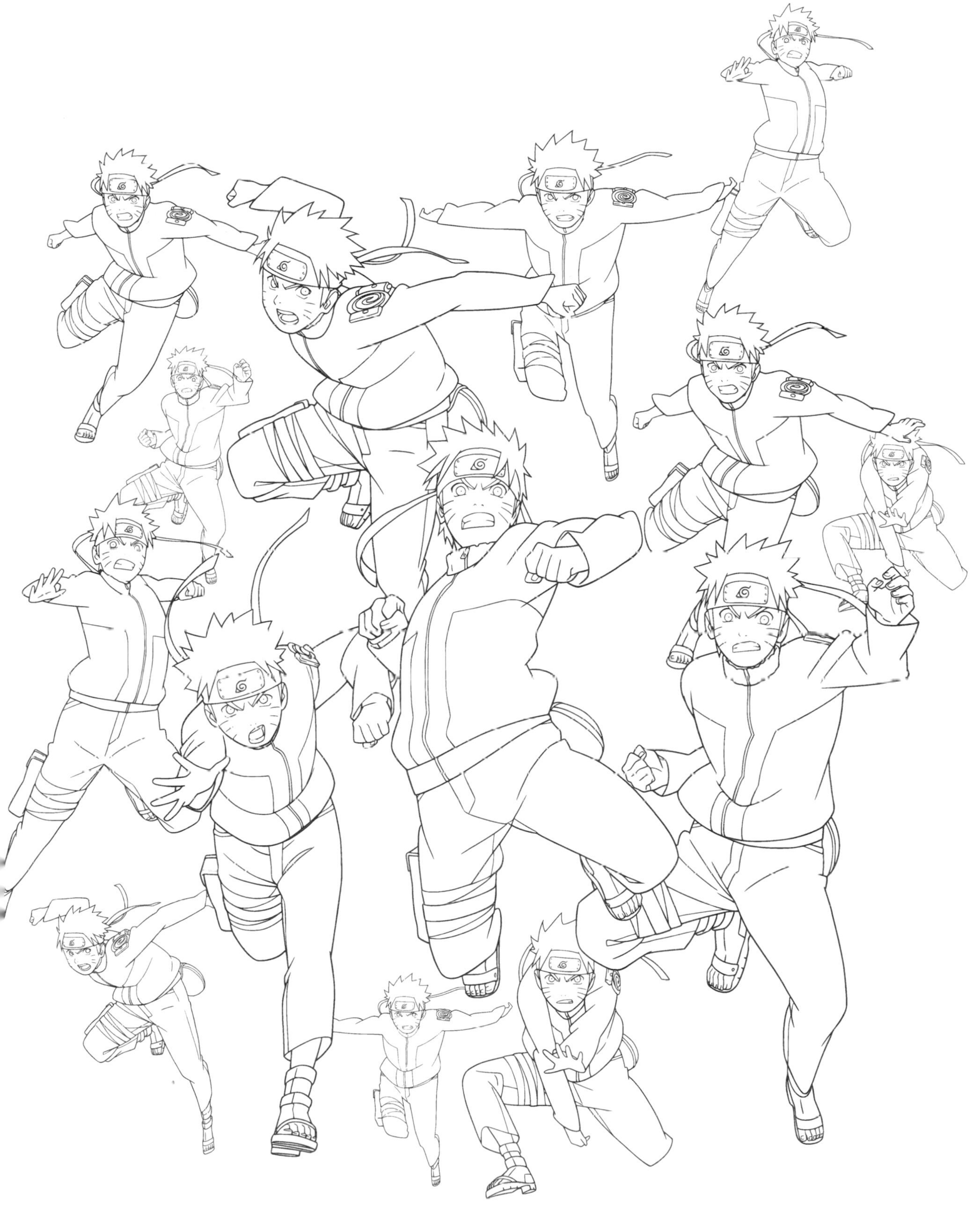

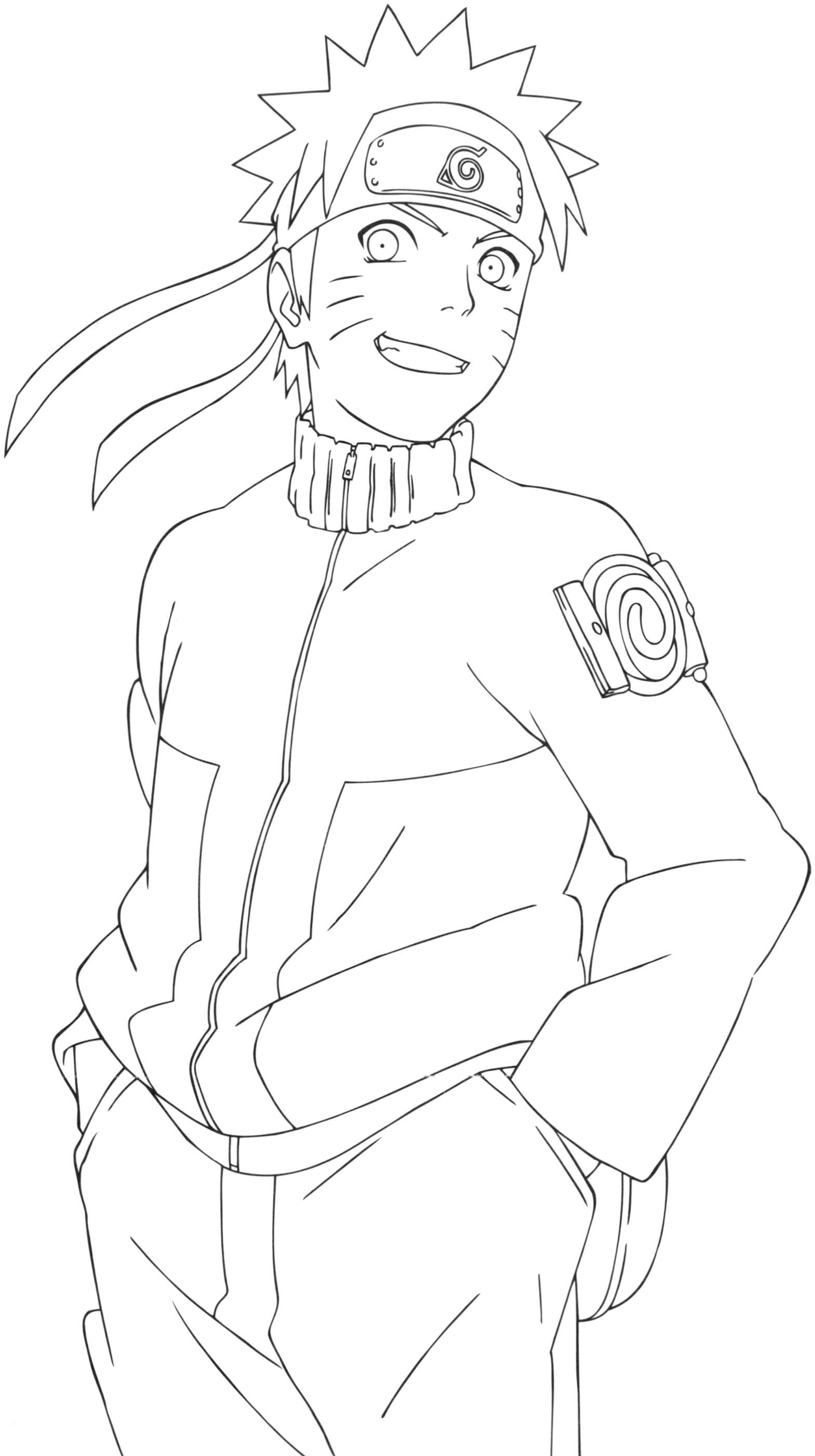

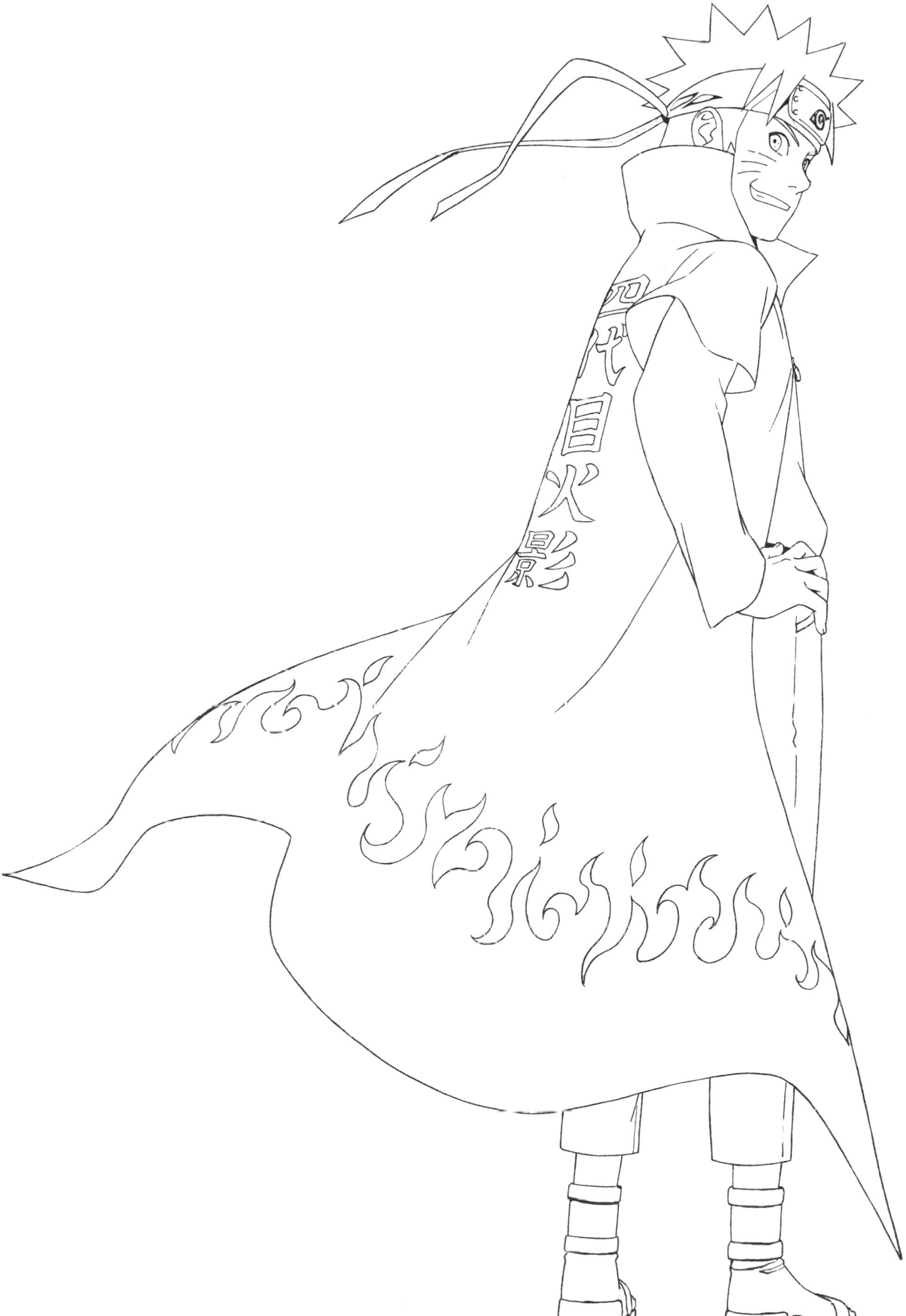
四代目火影

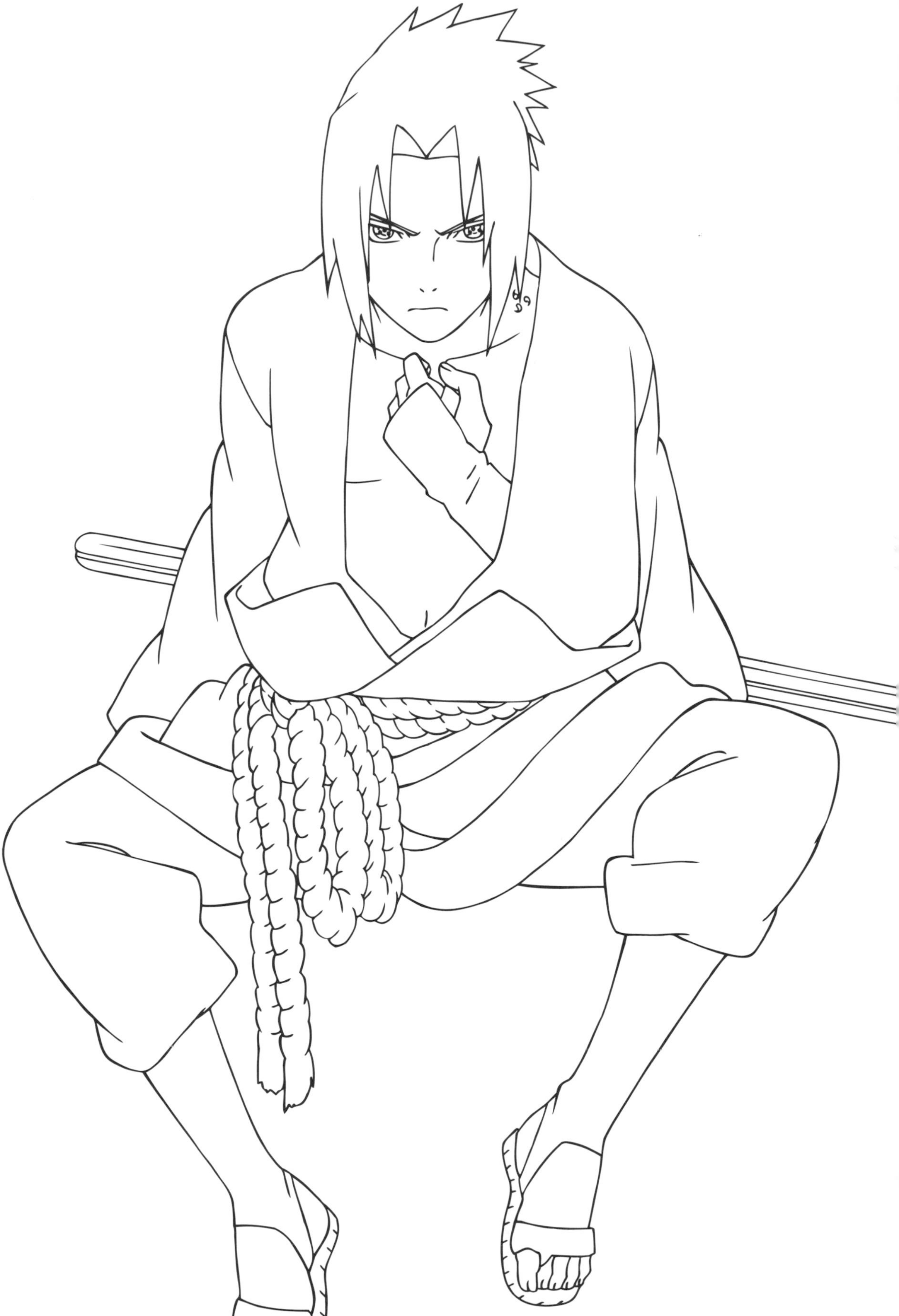

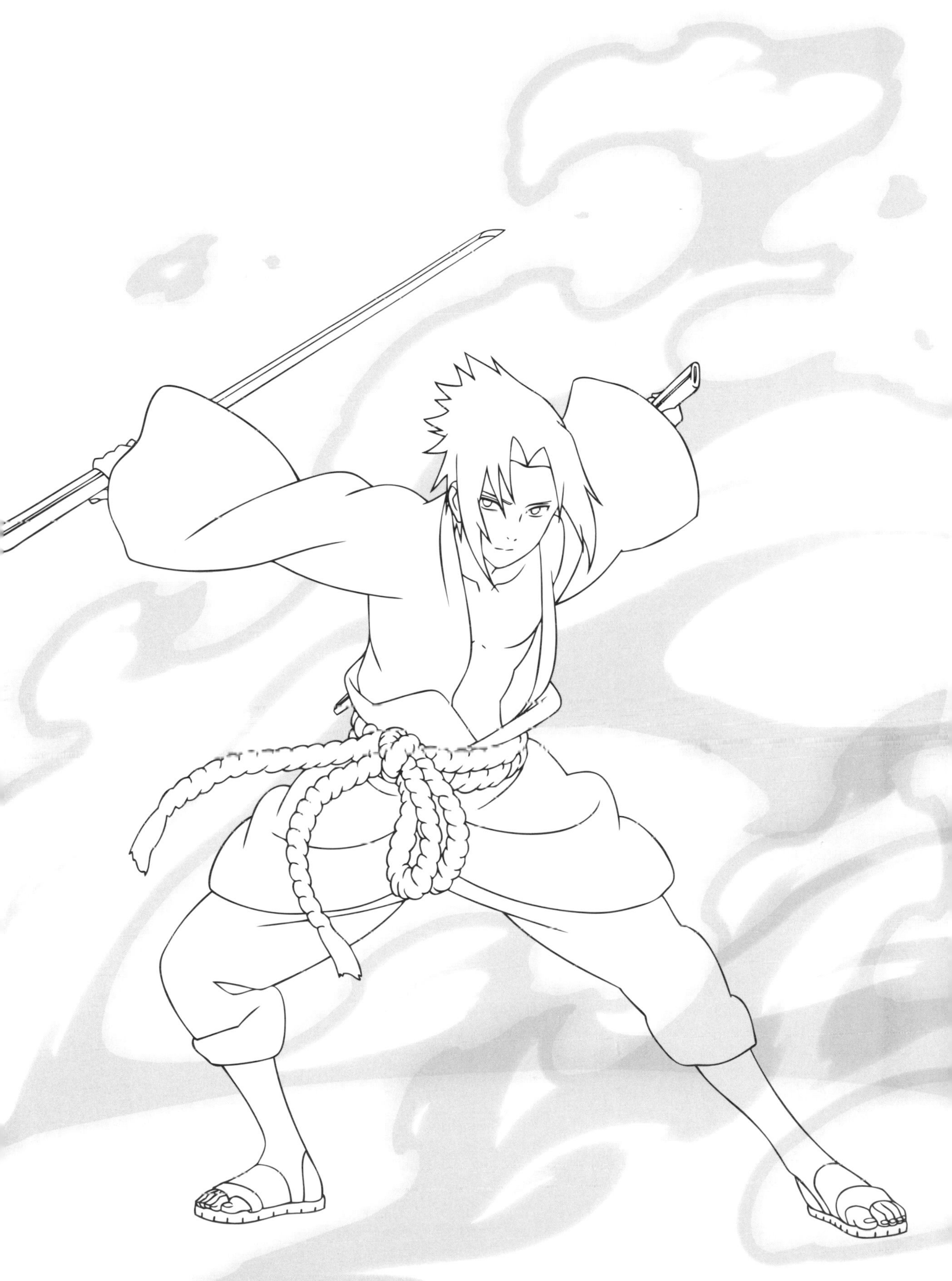

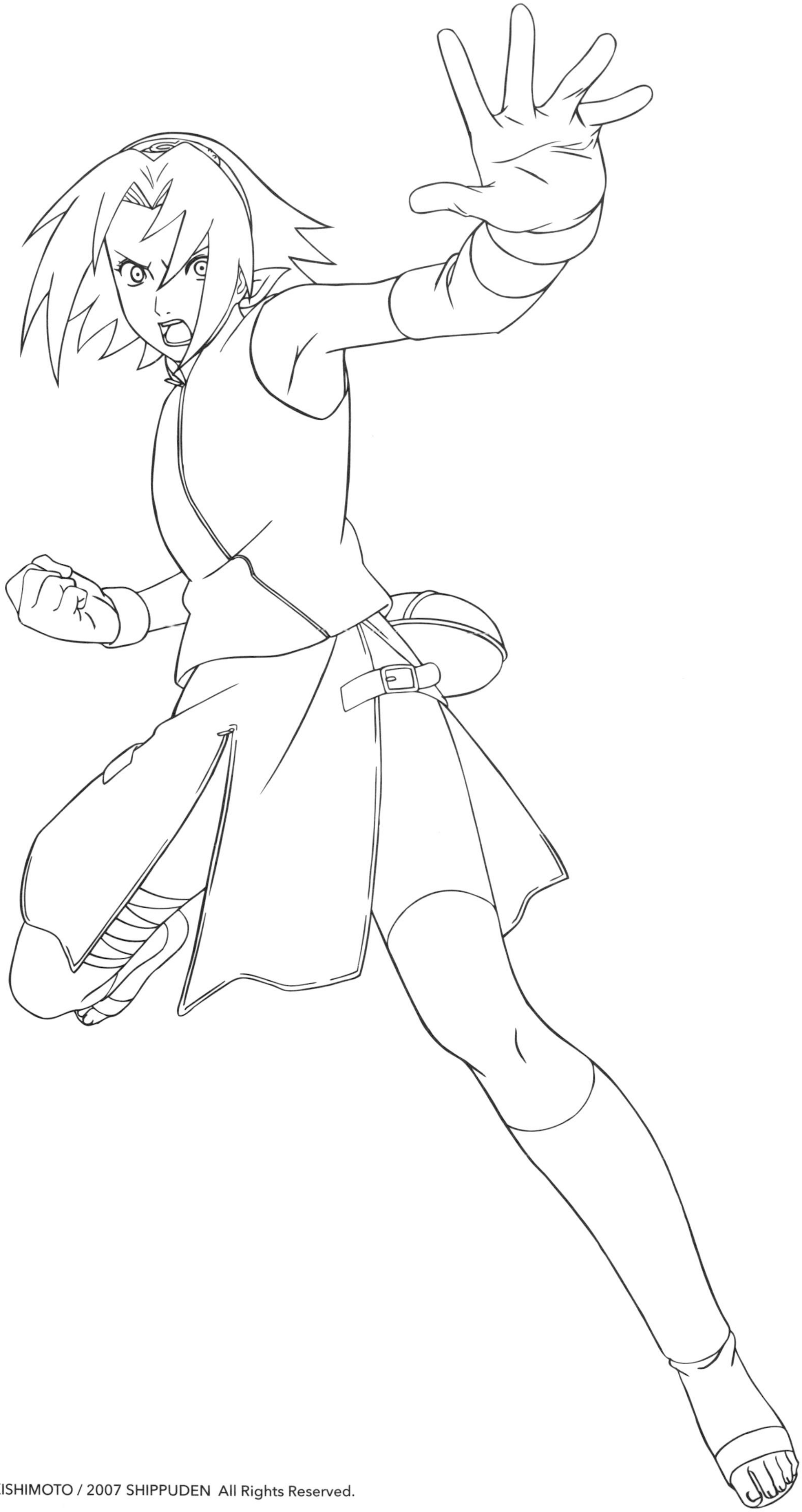

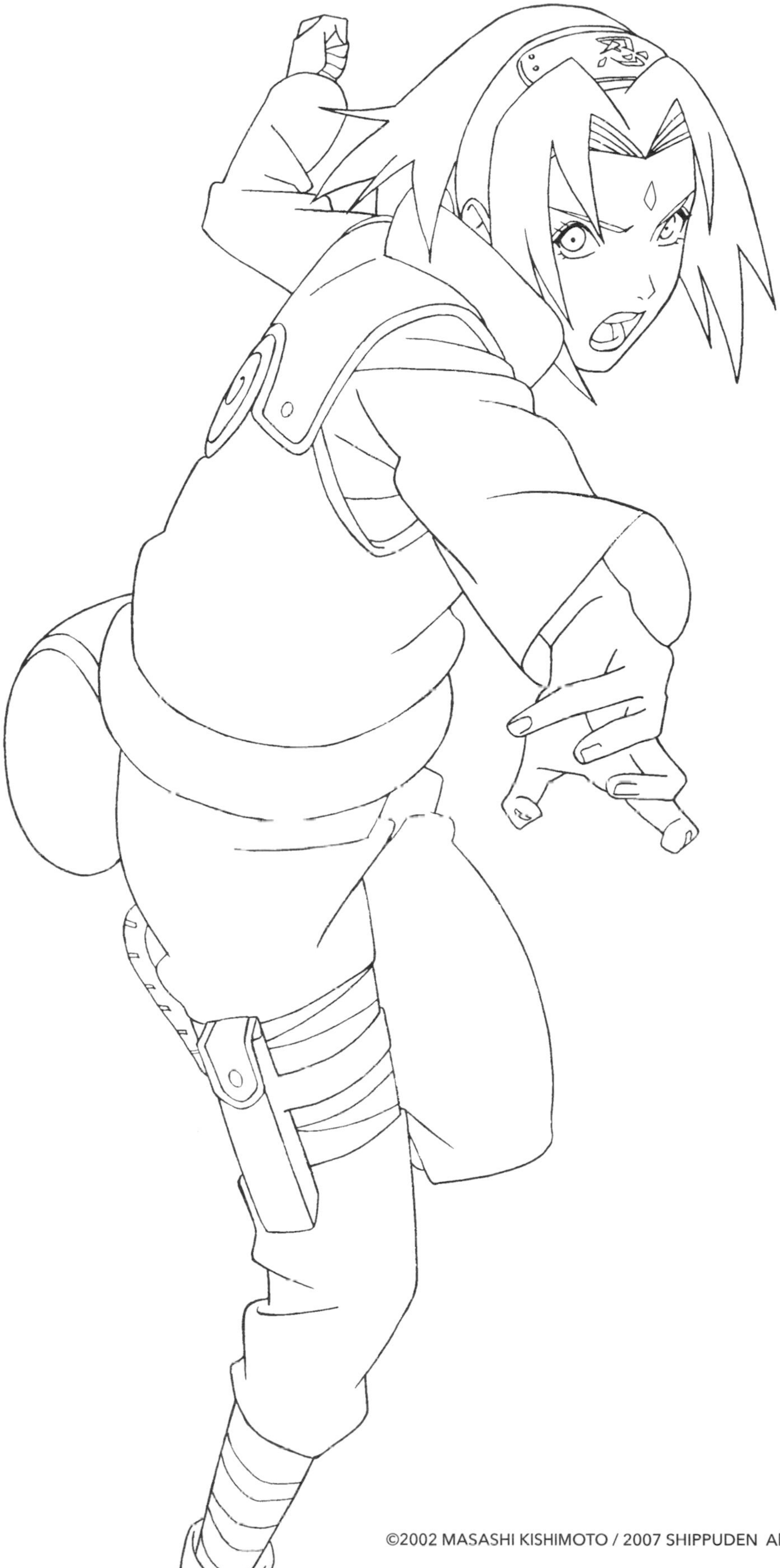

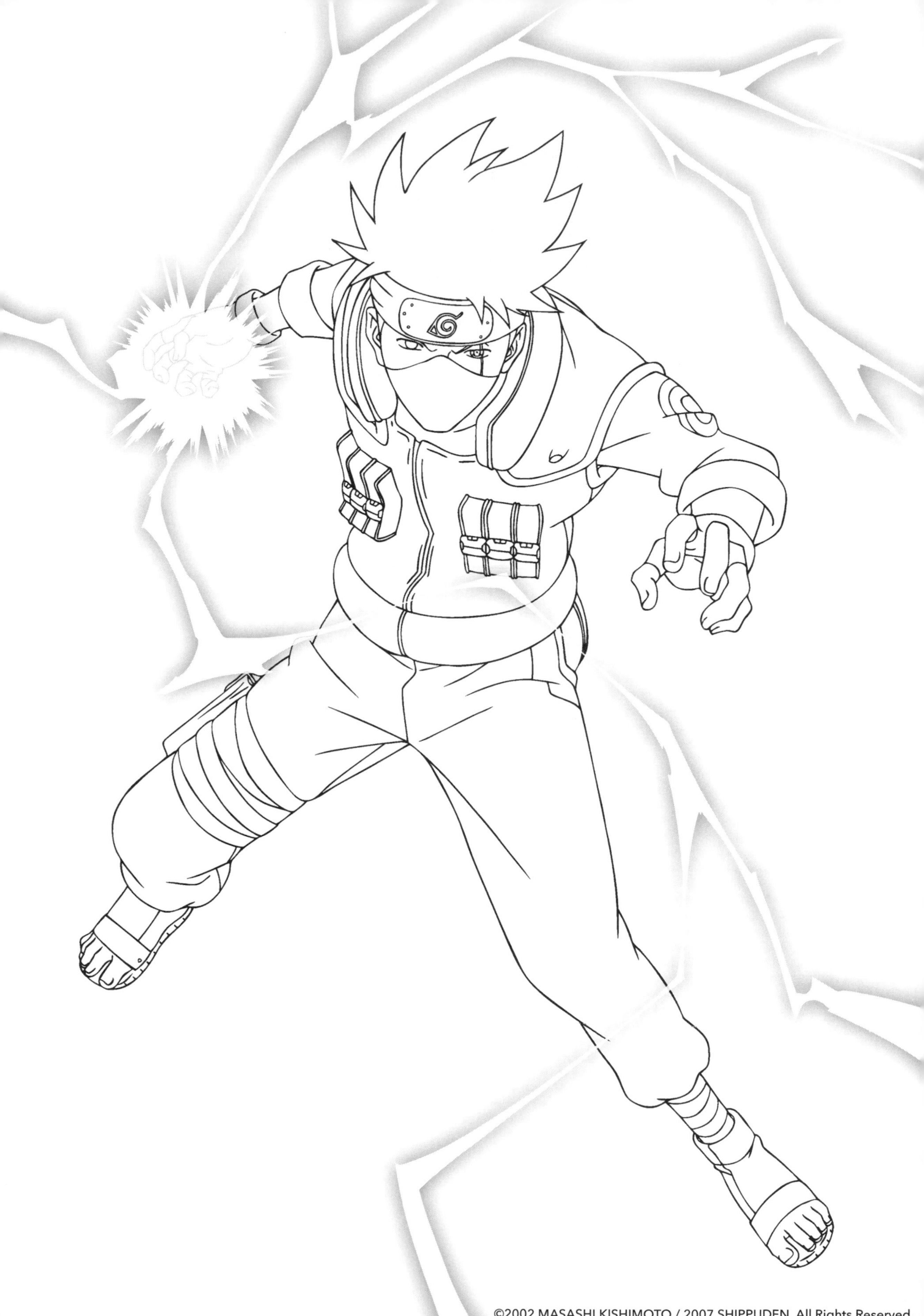

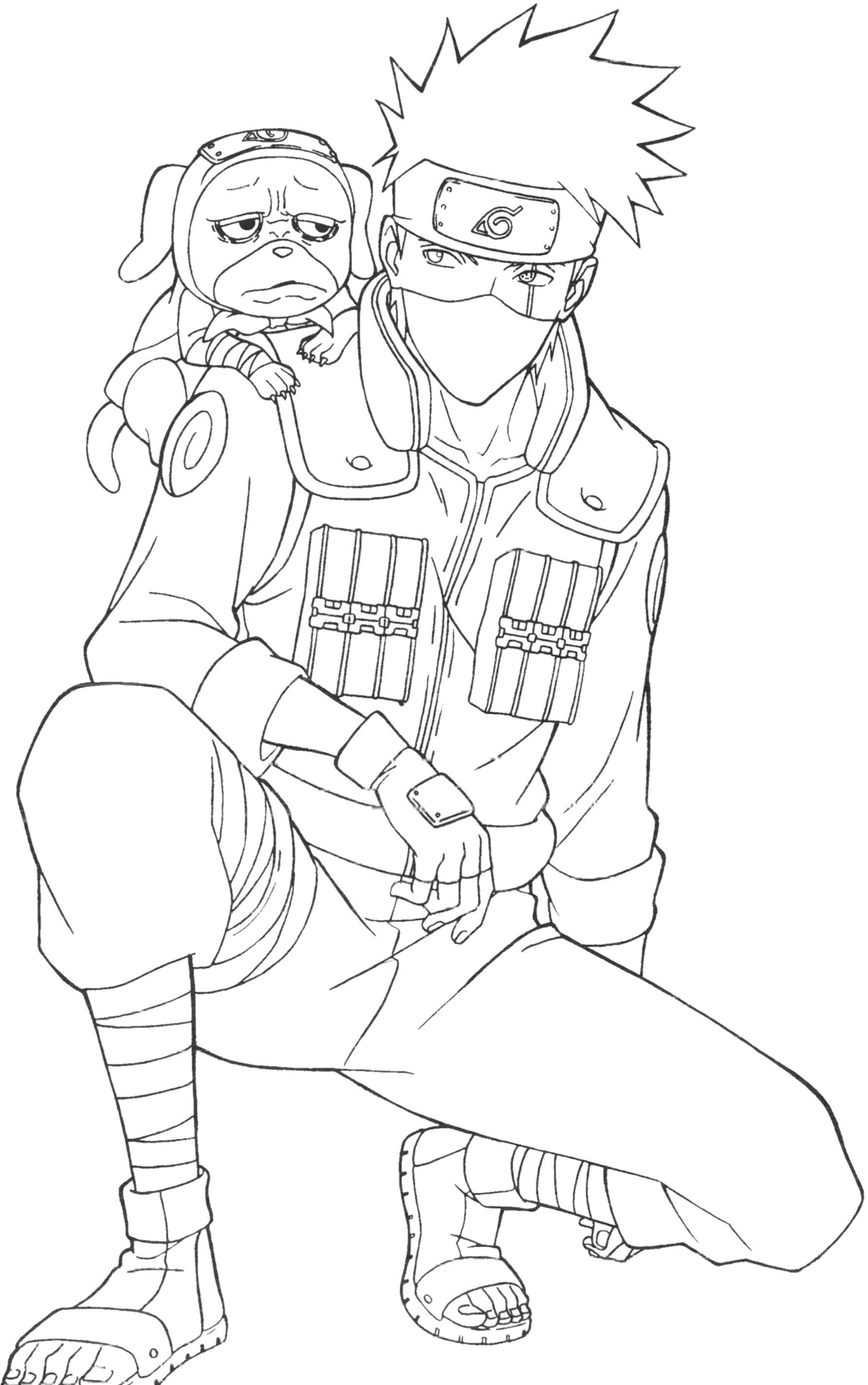

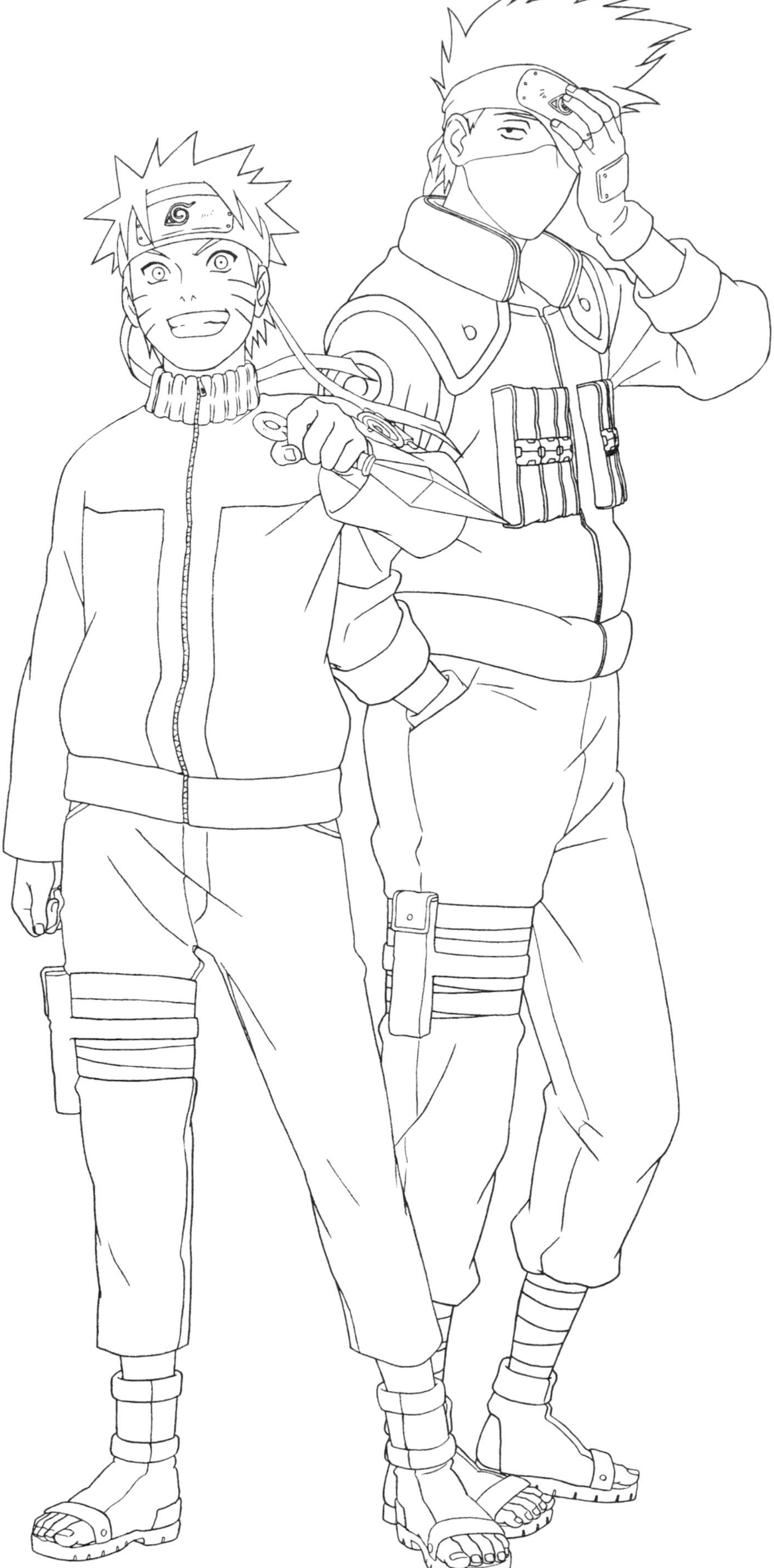

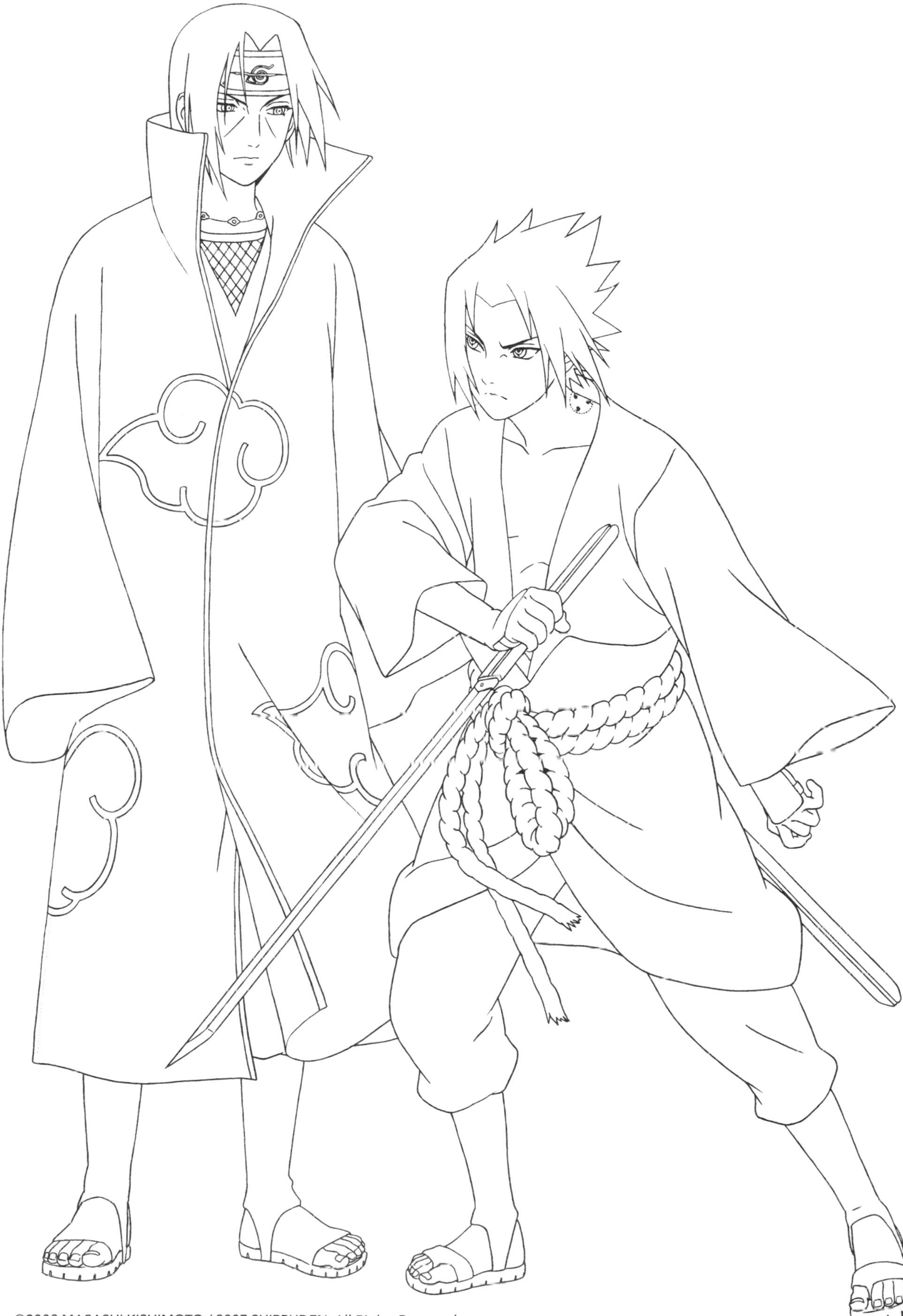

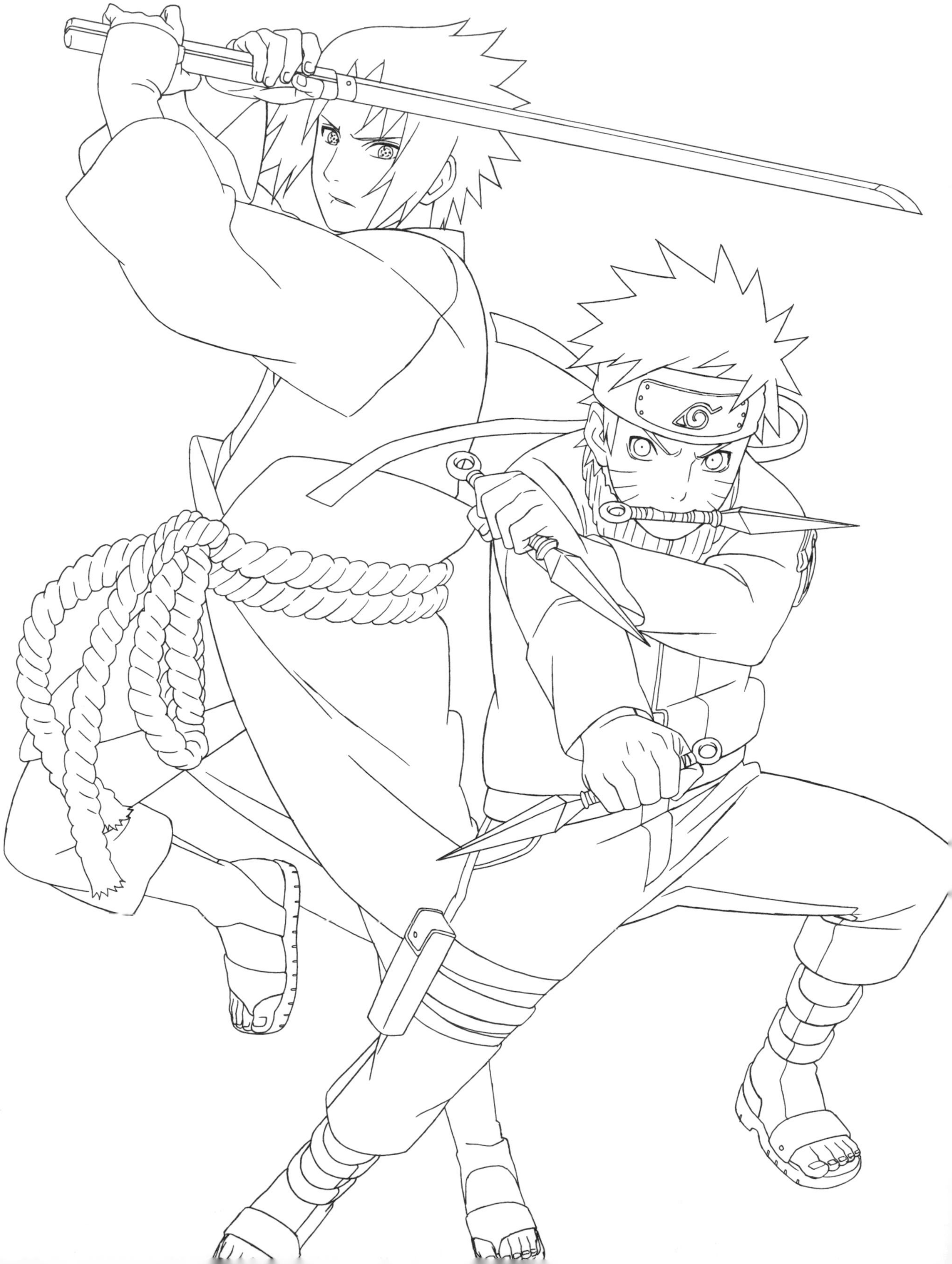

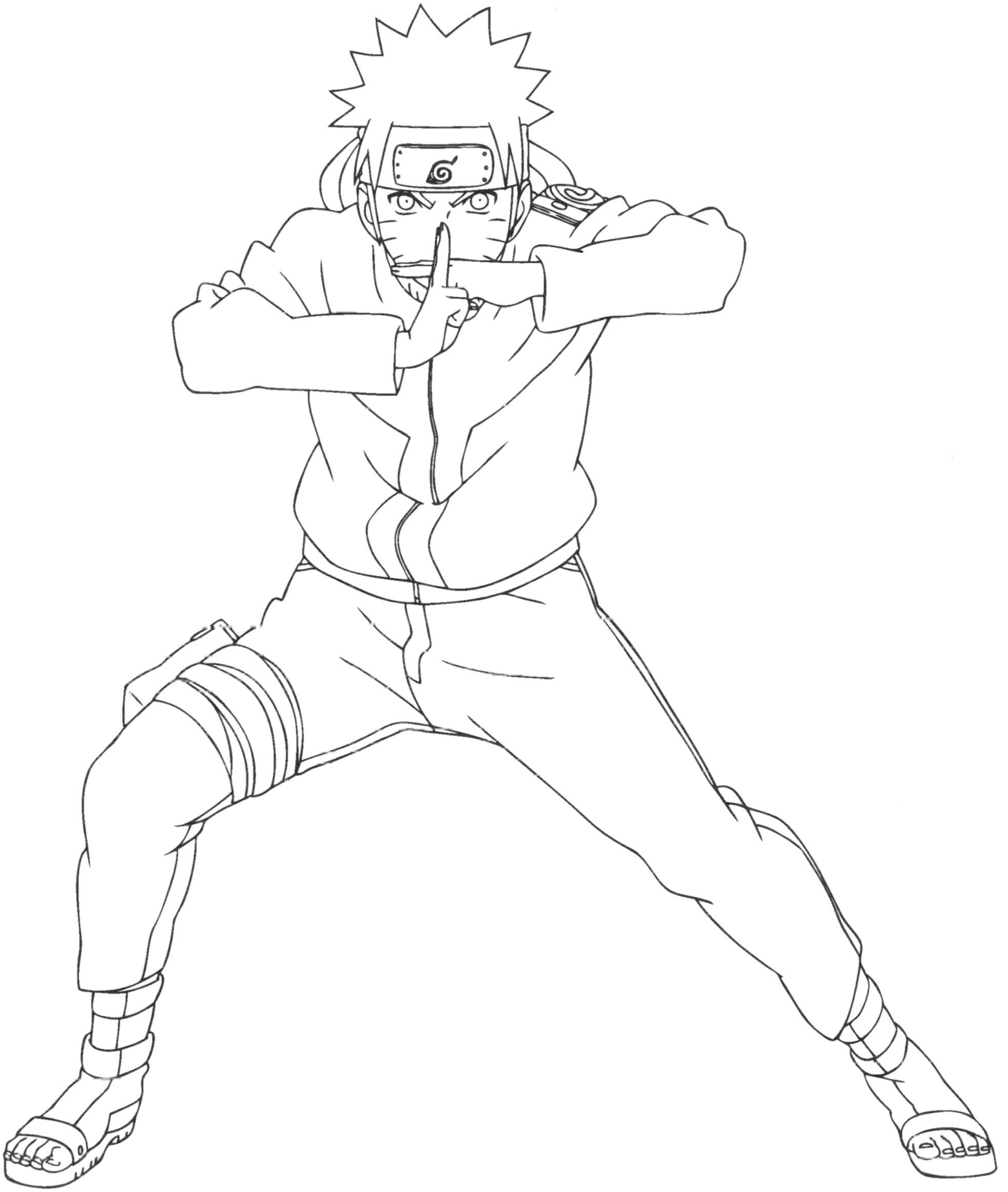

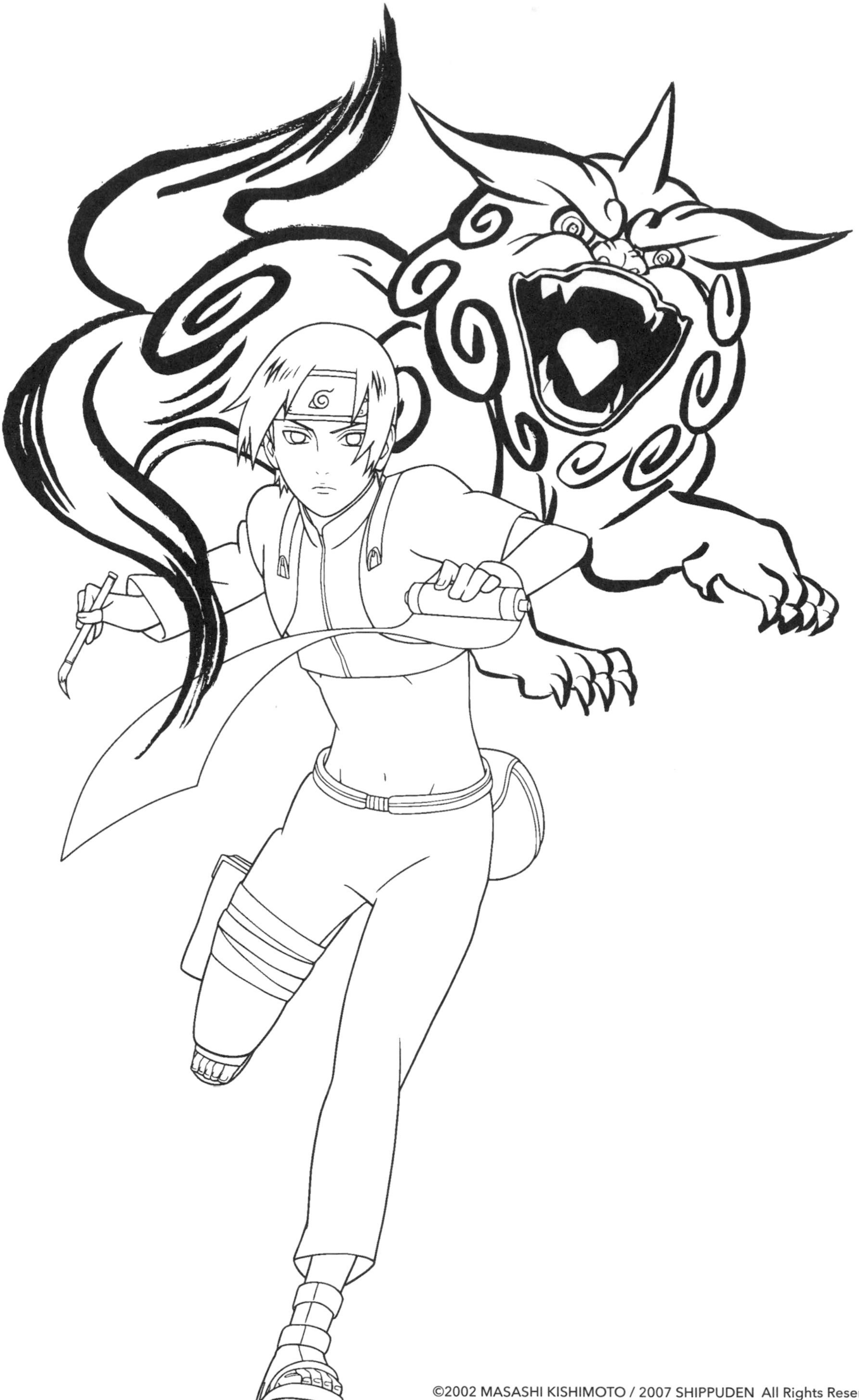

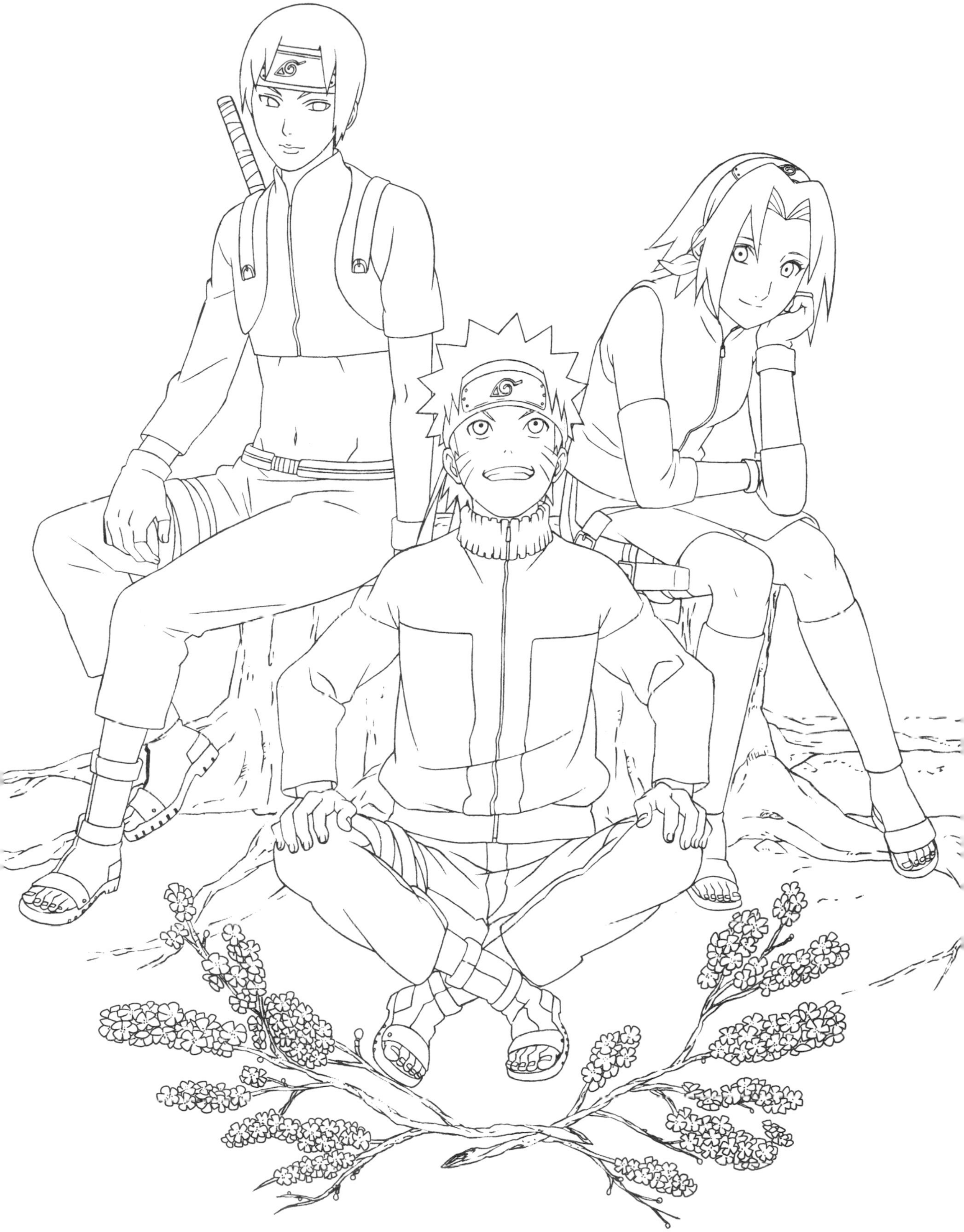

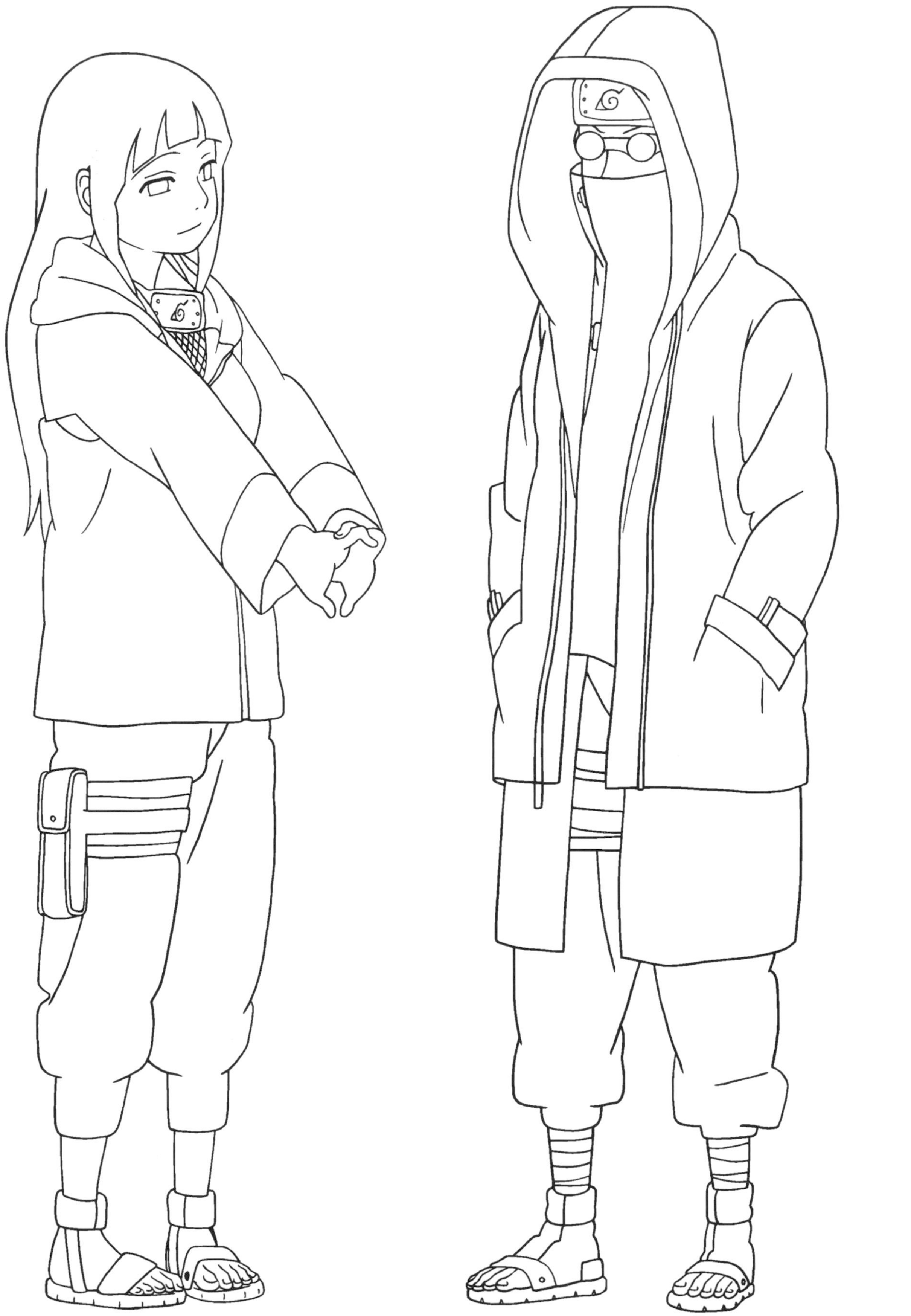

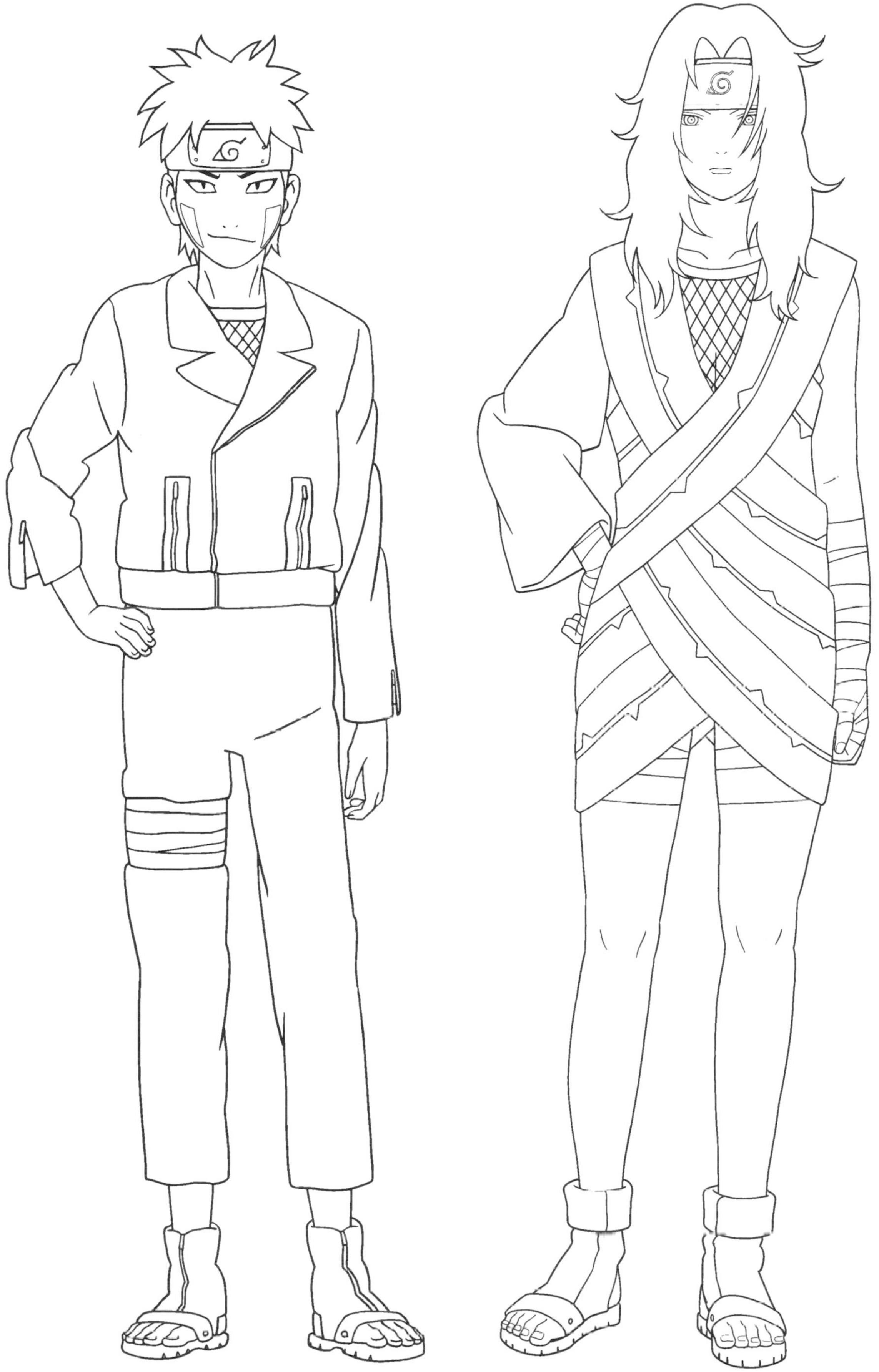

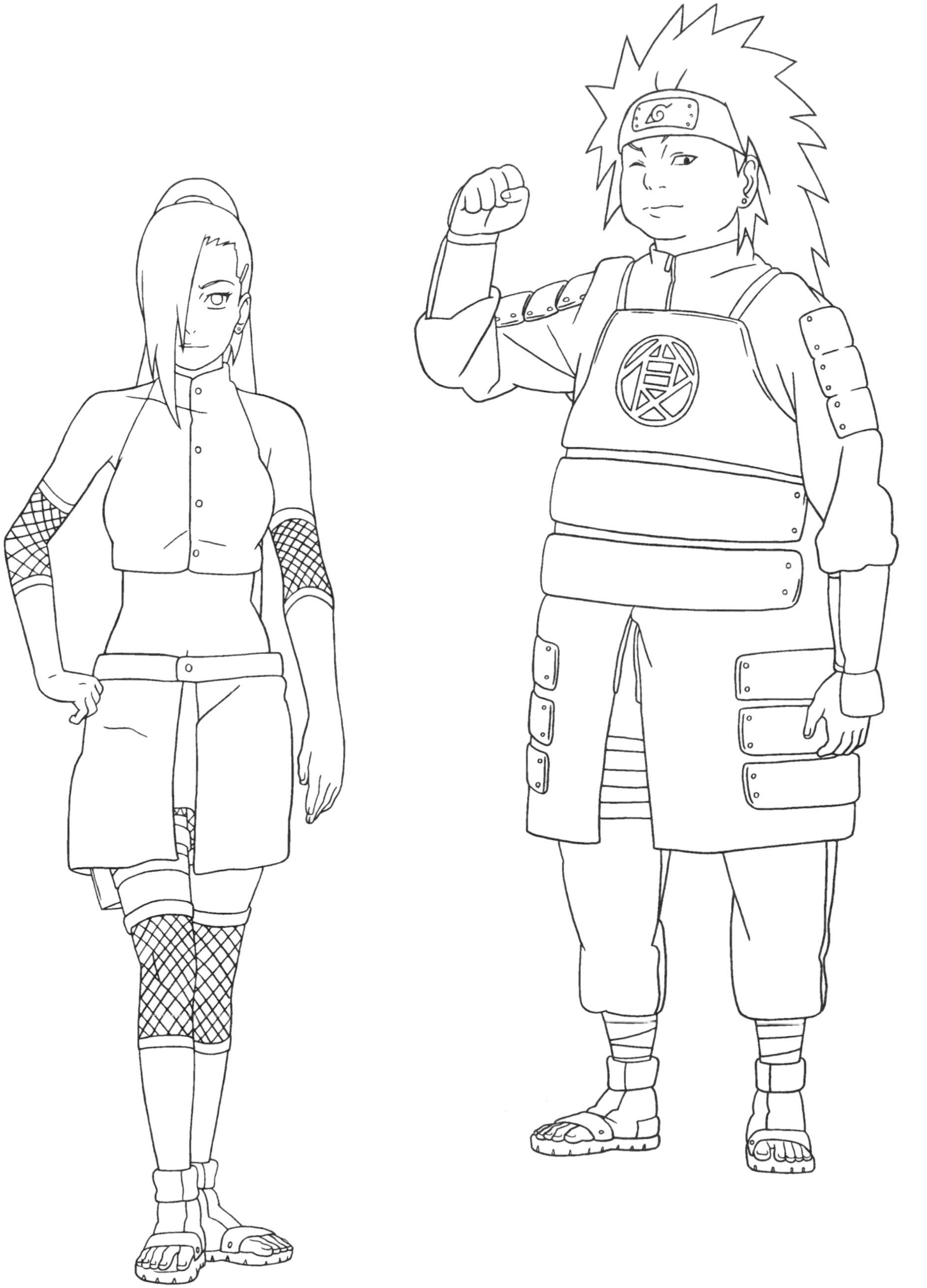

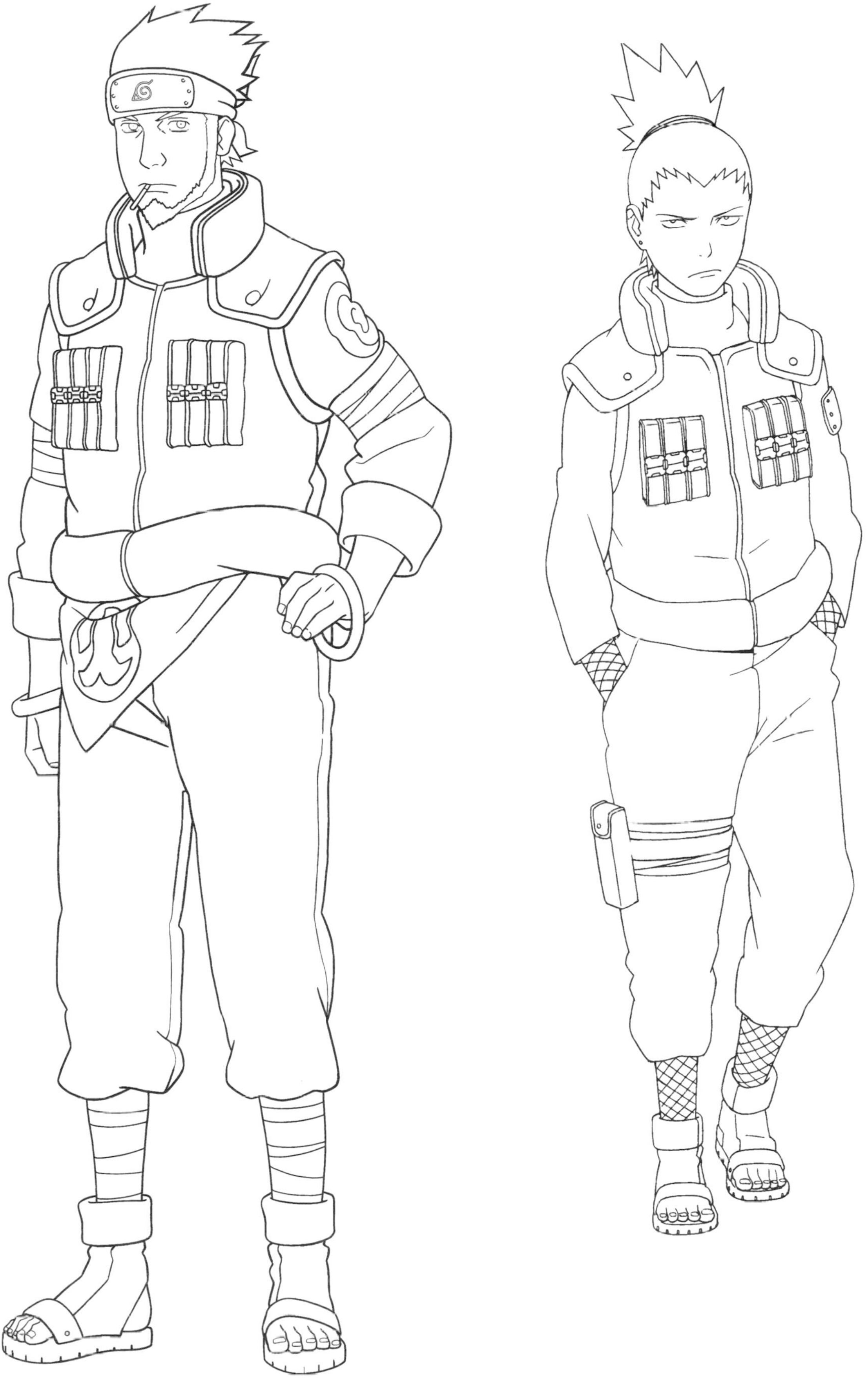

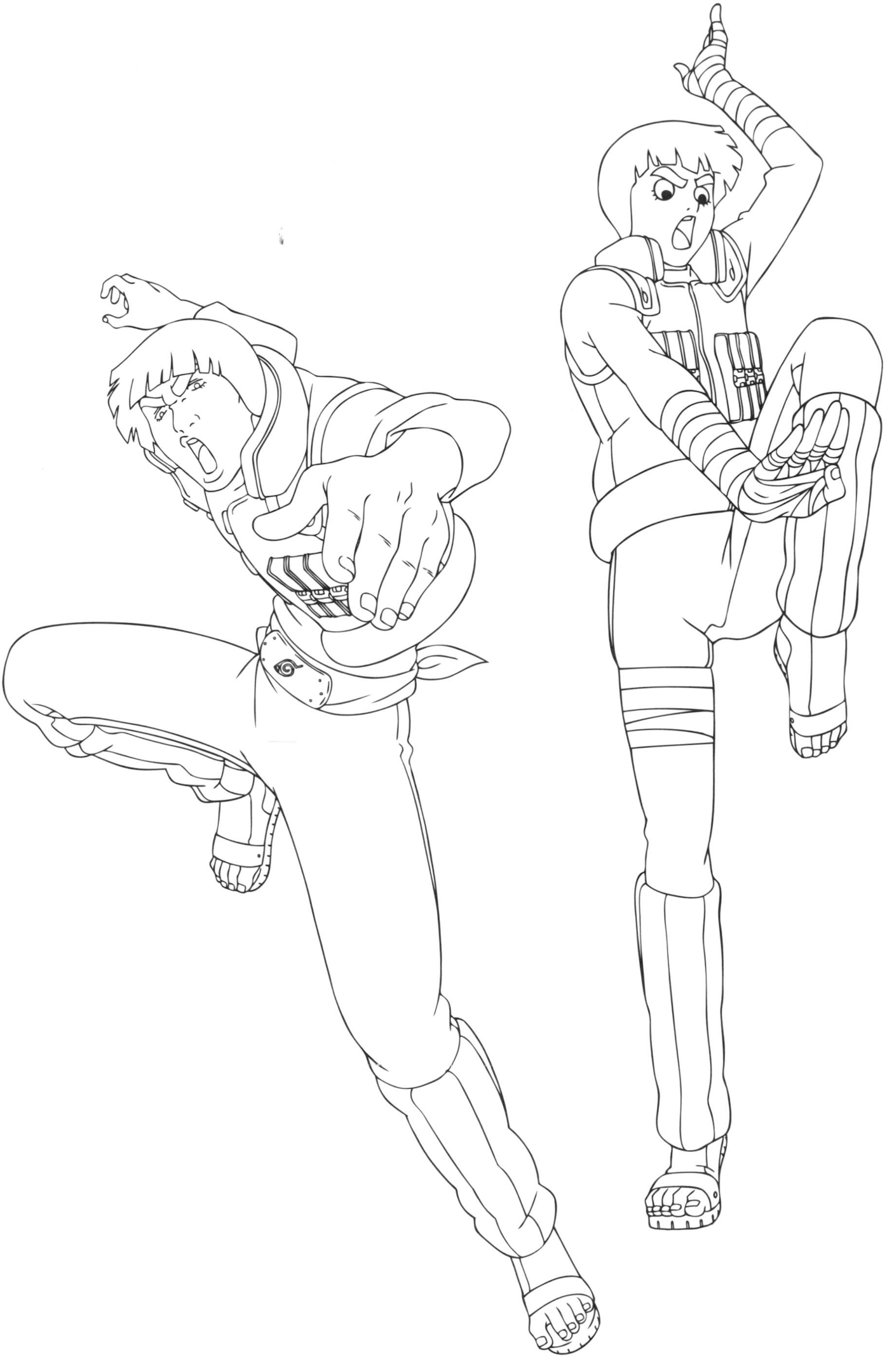

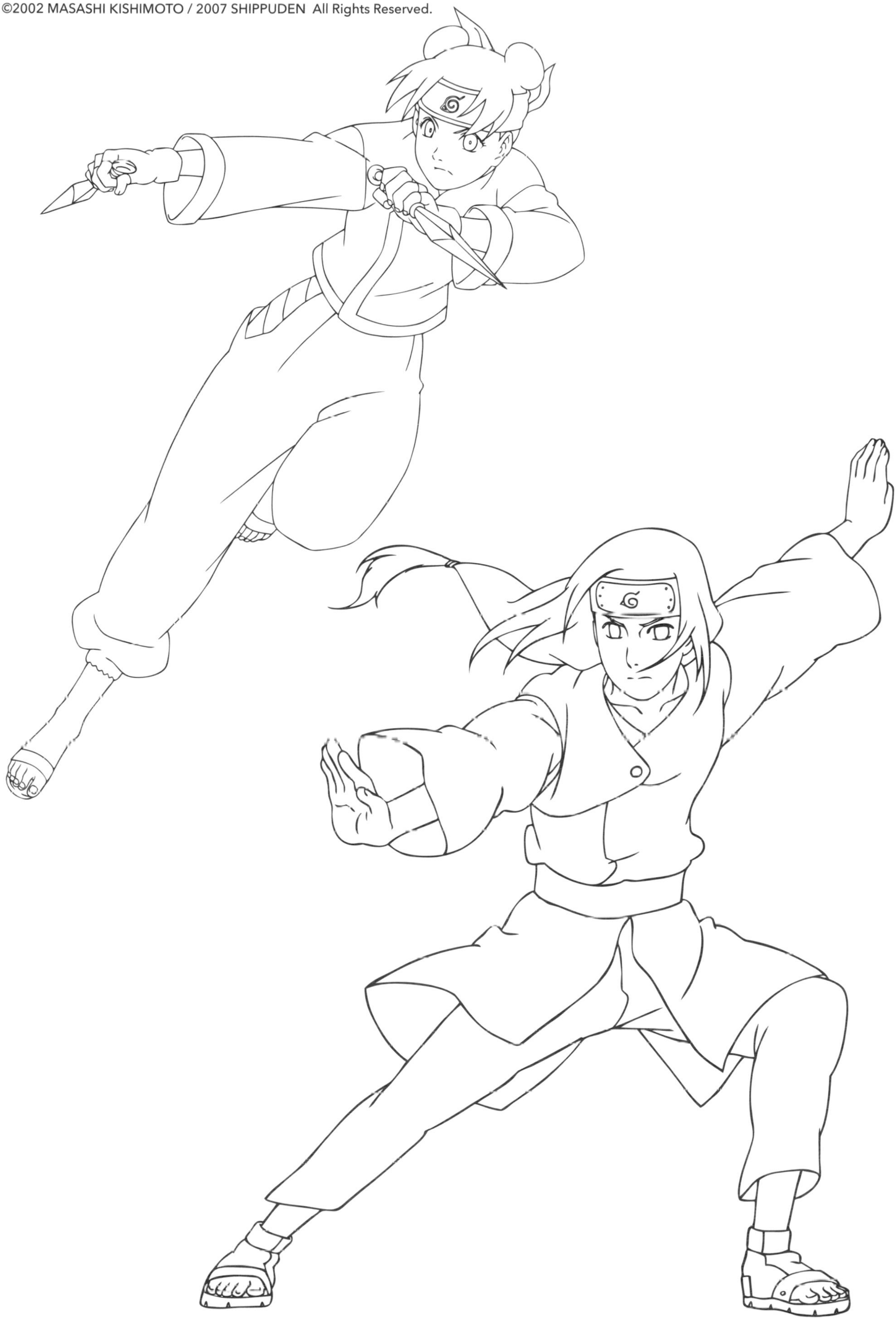

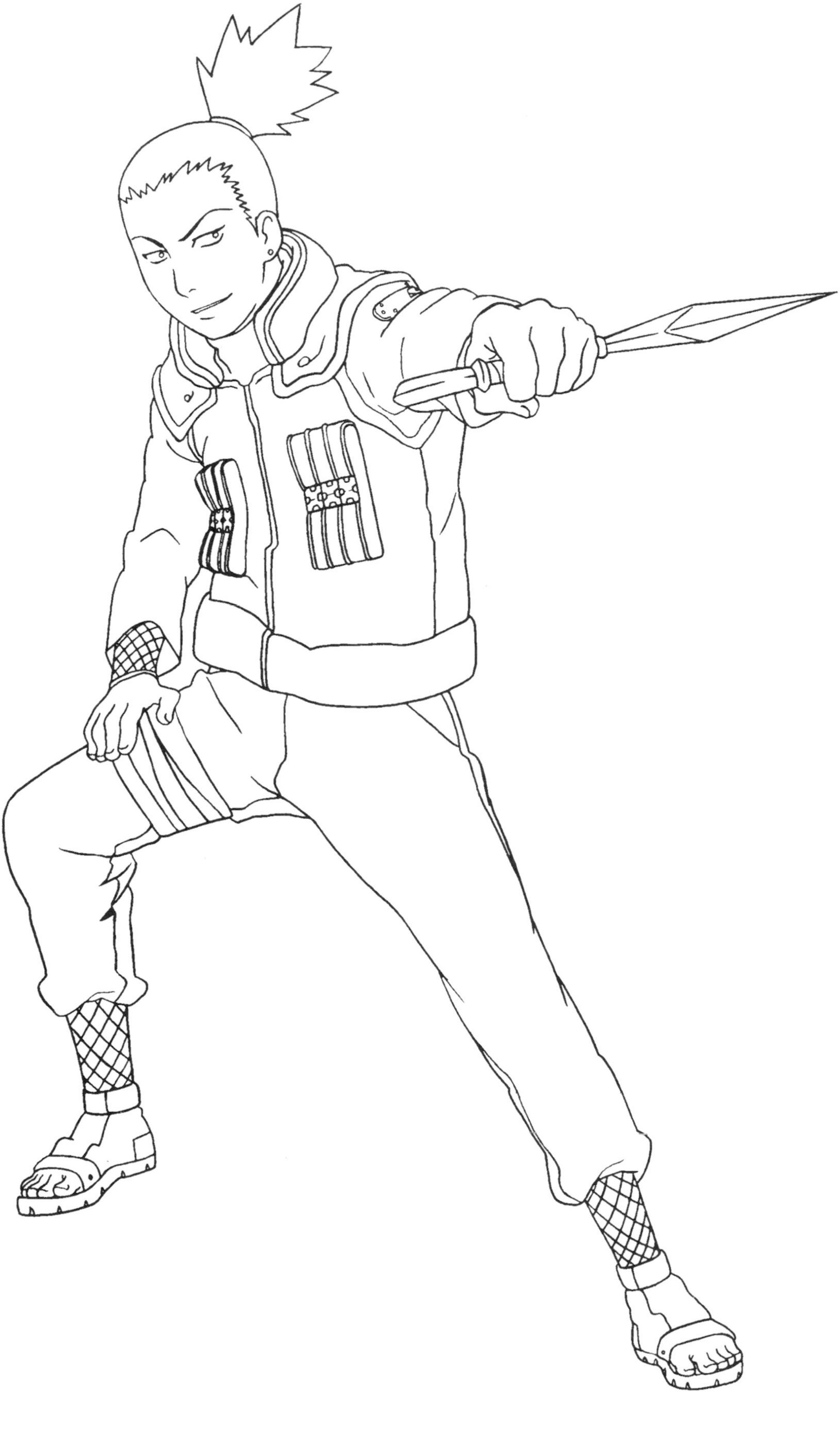

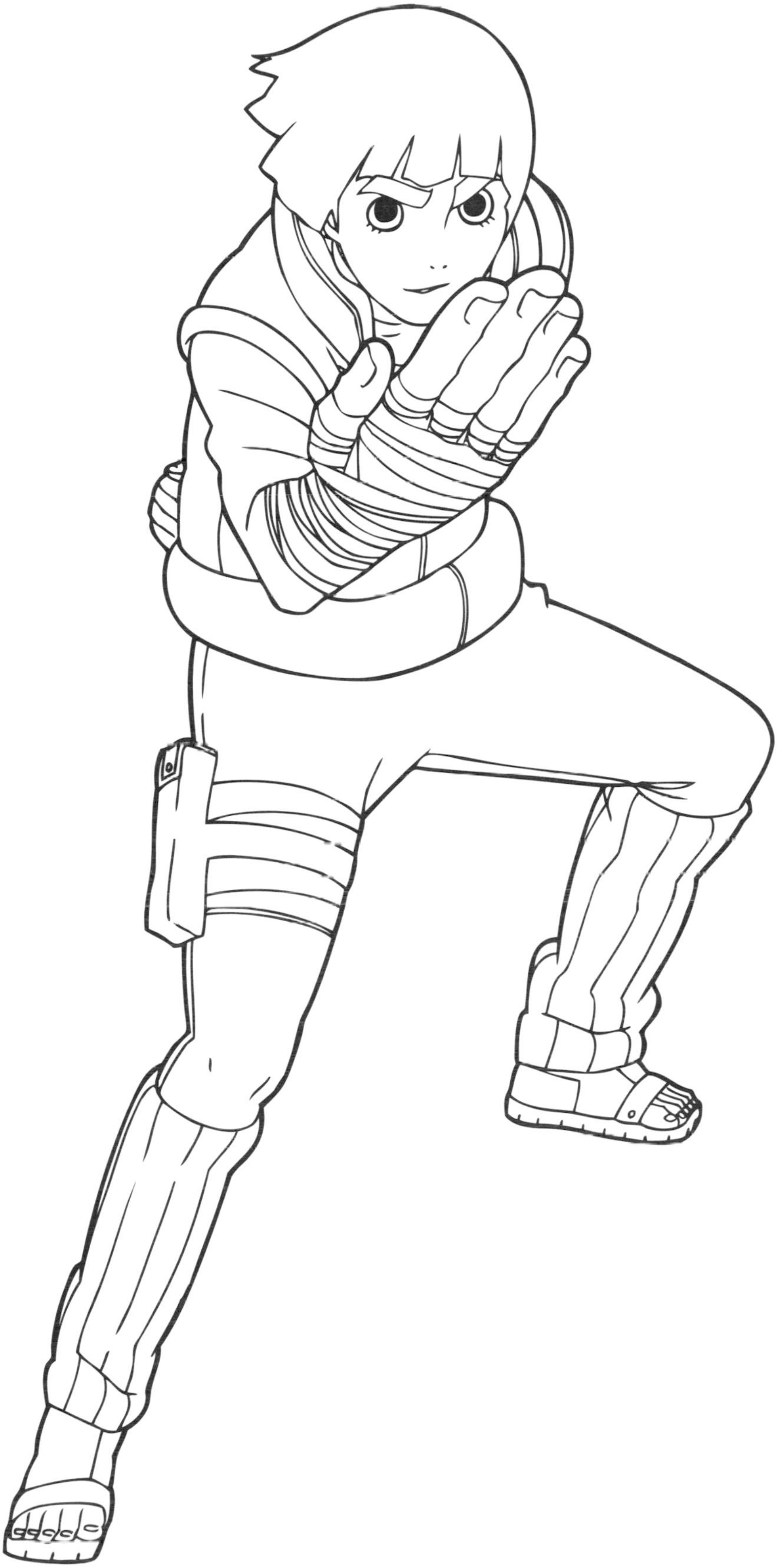

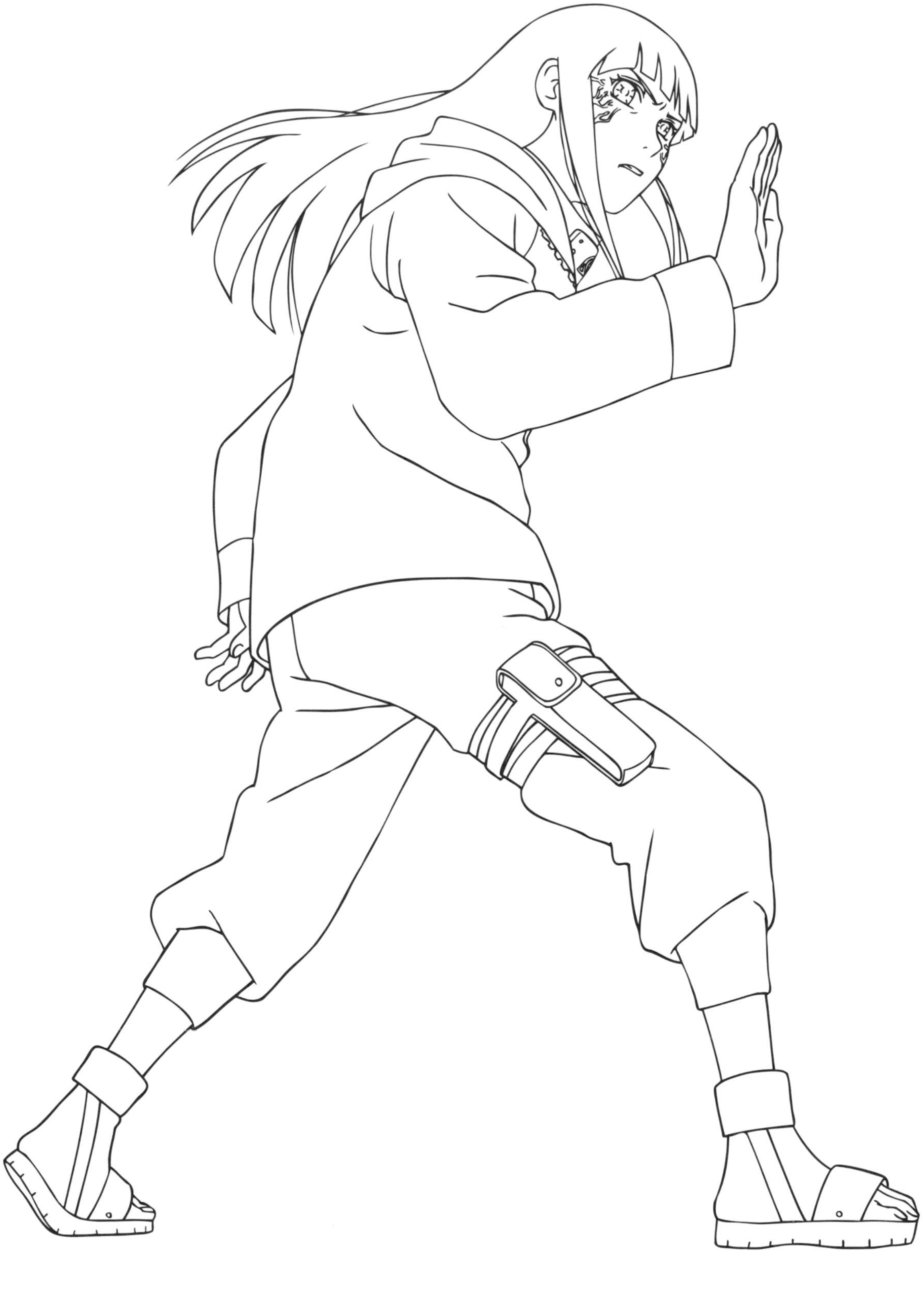

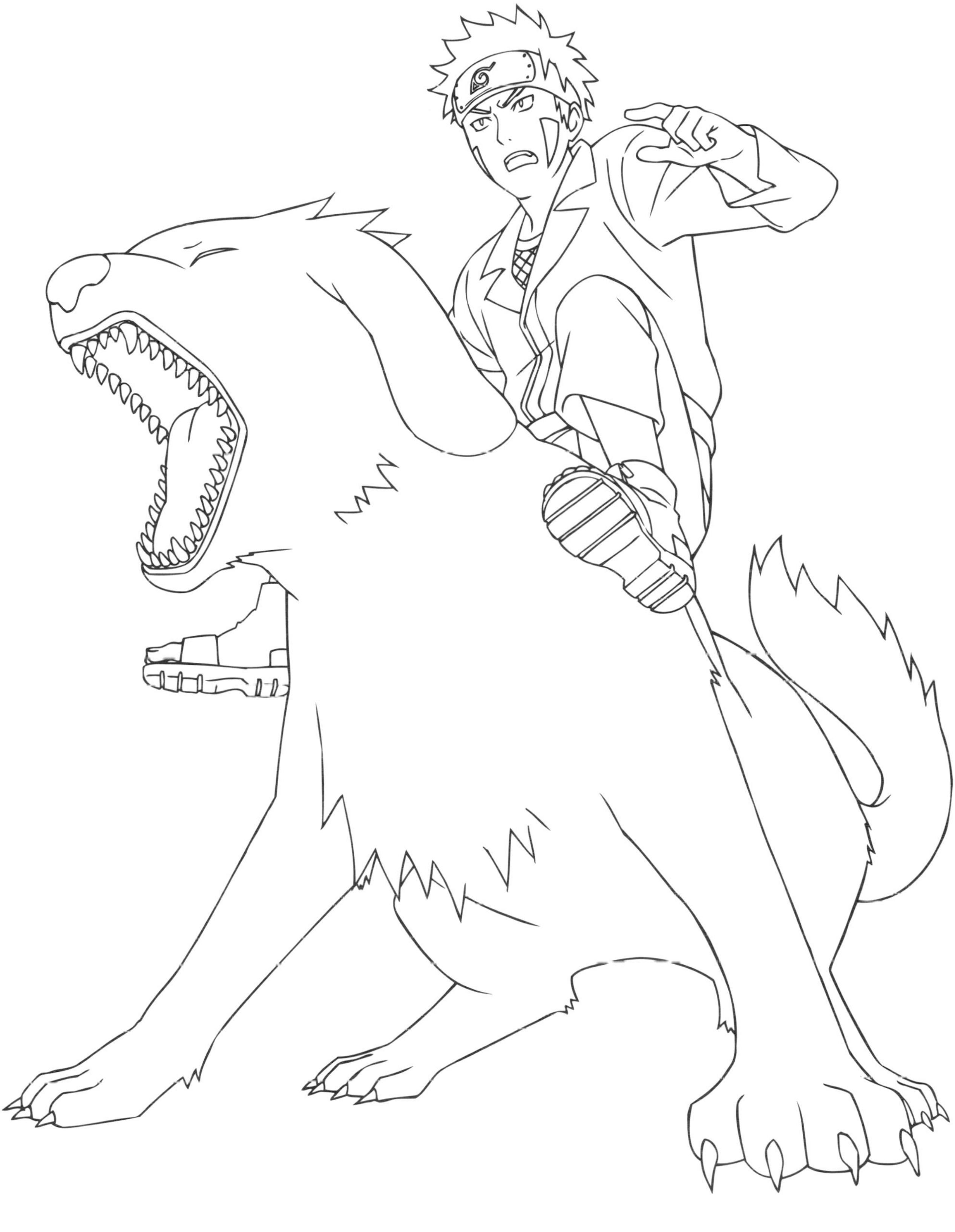

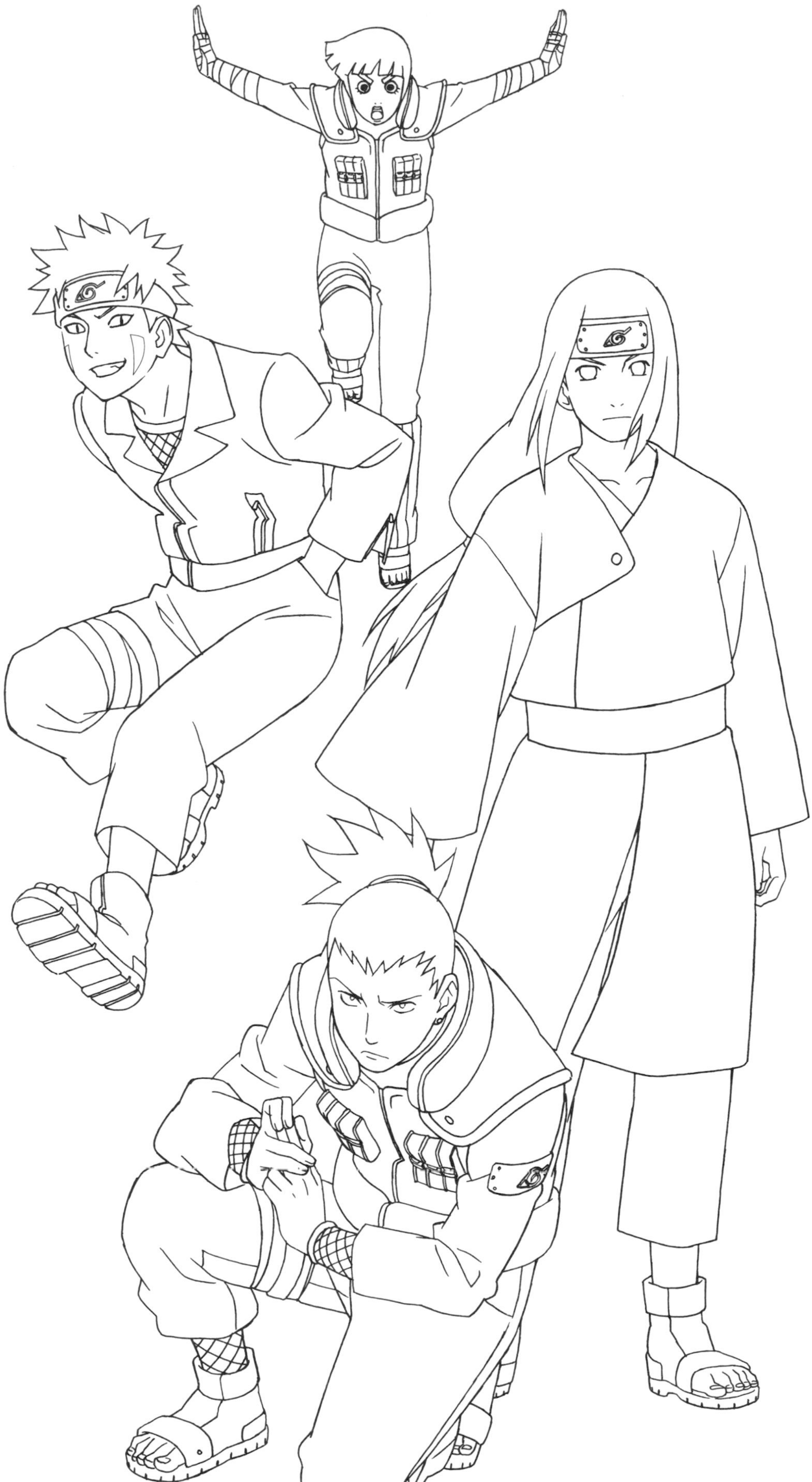

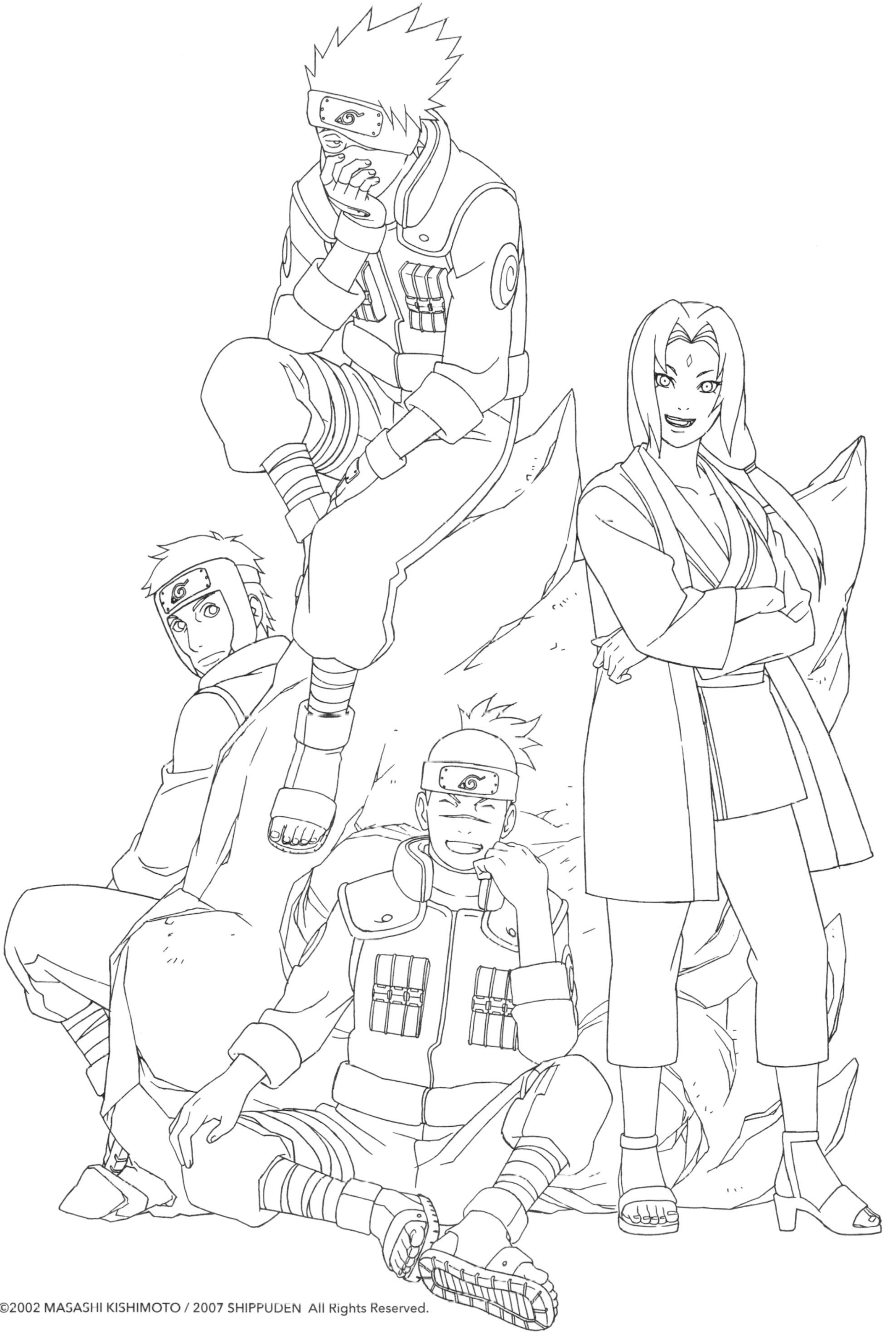

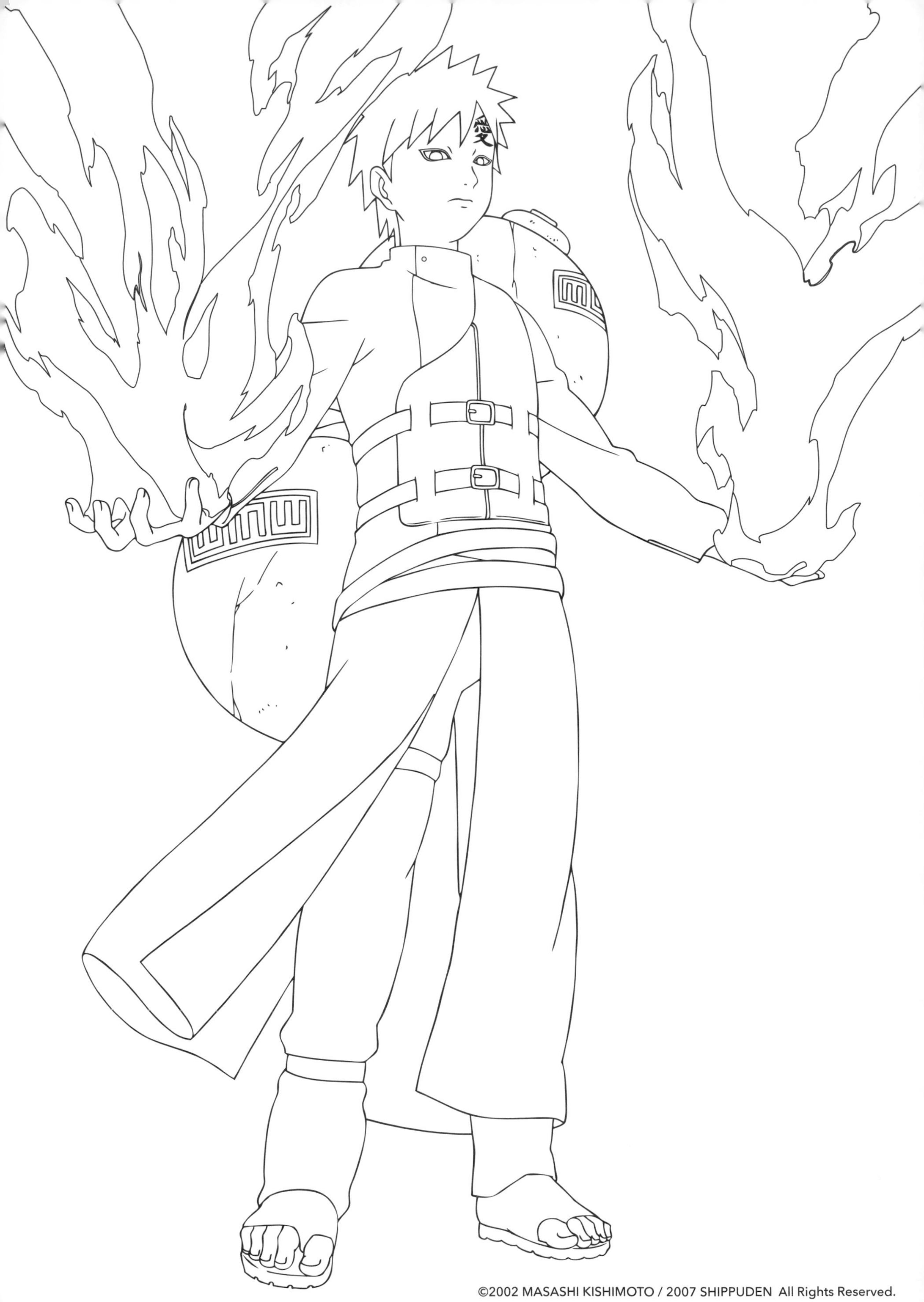

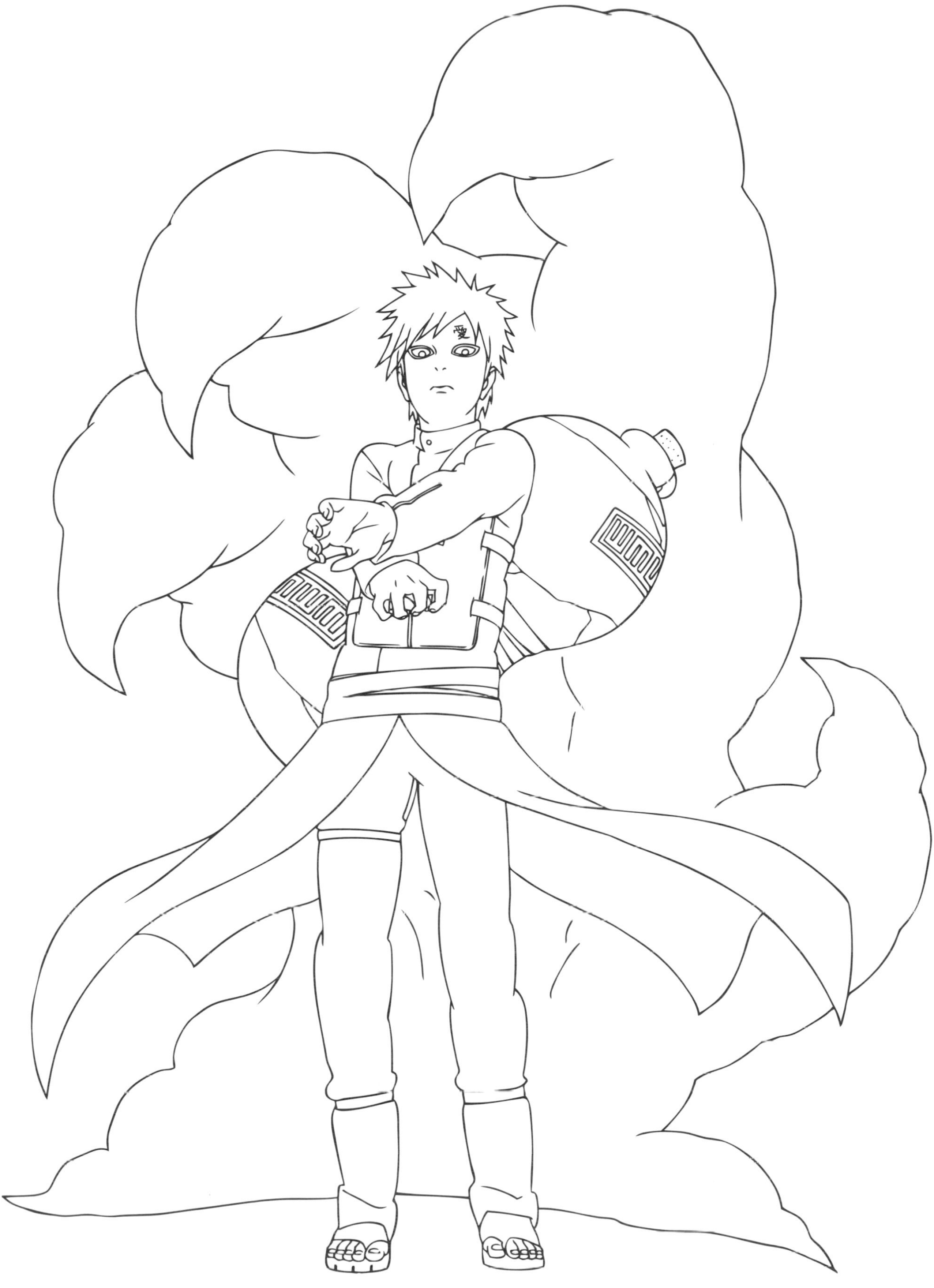
愛

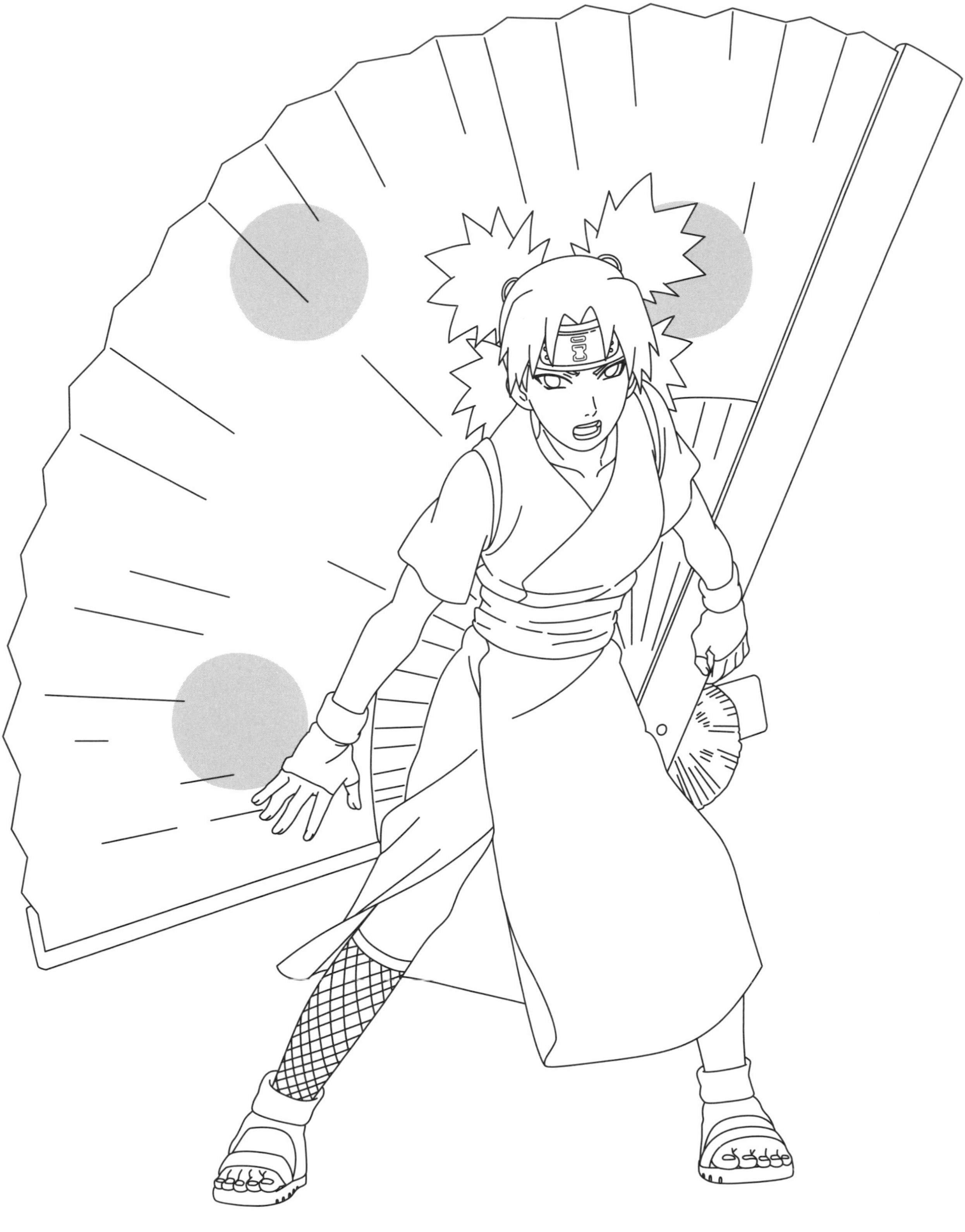

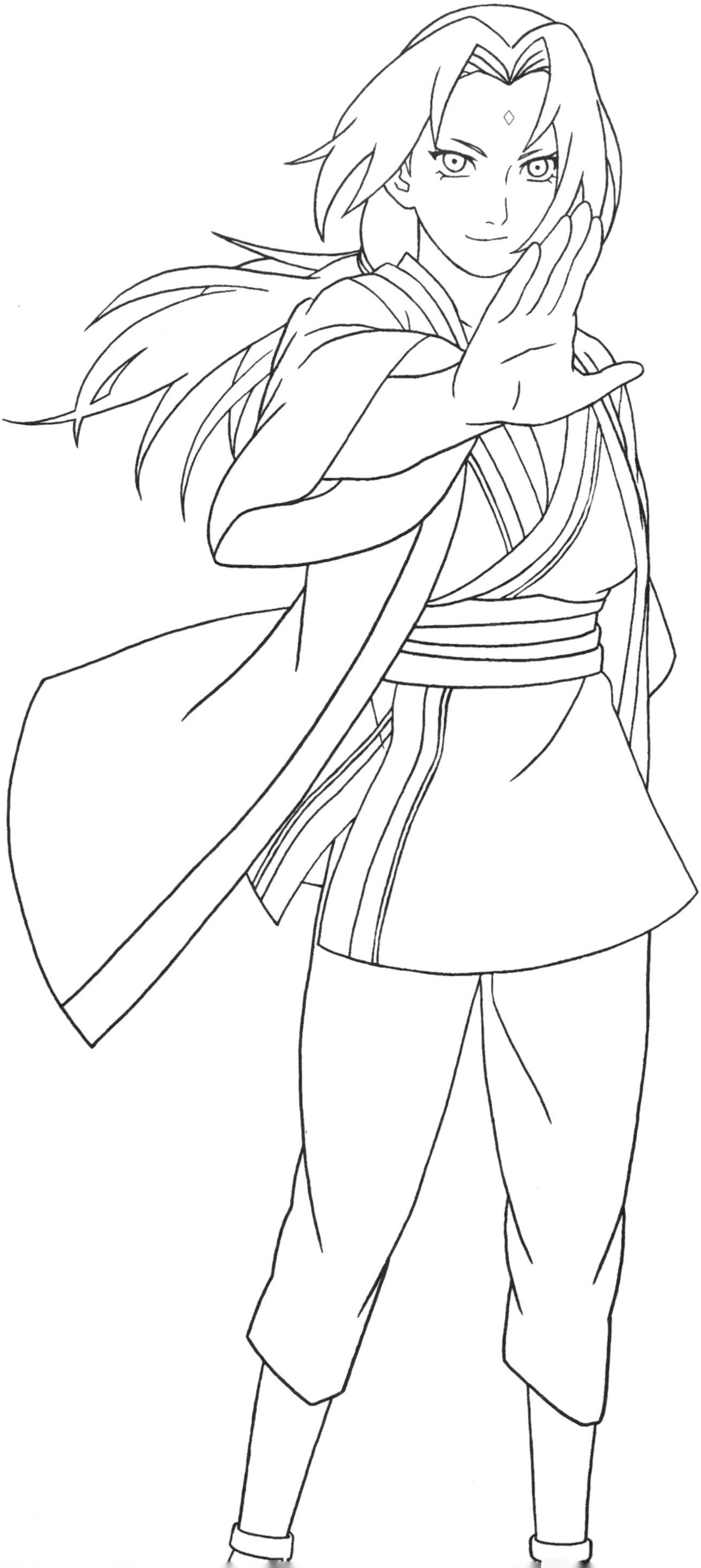

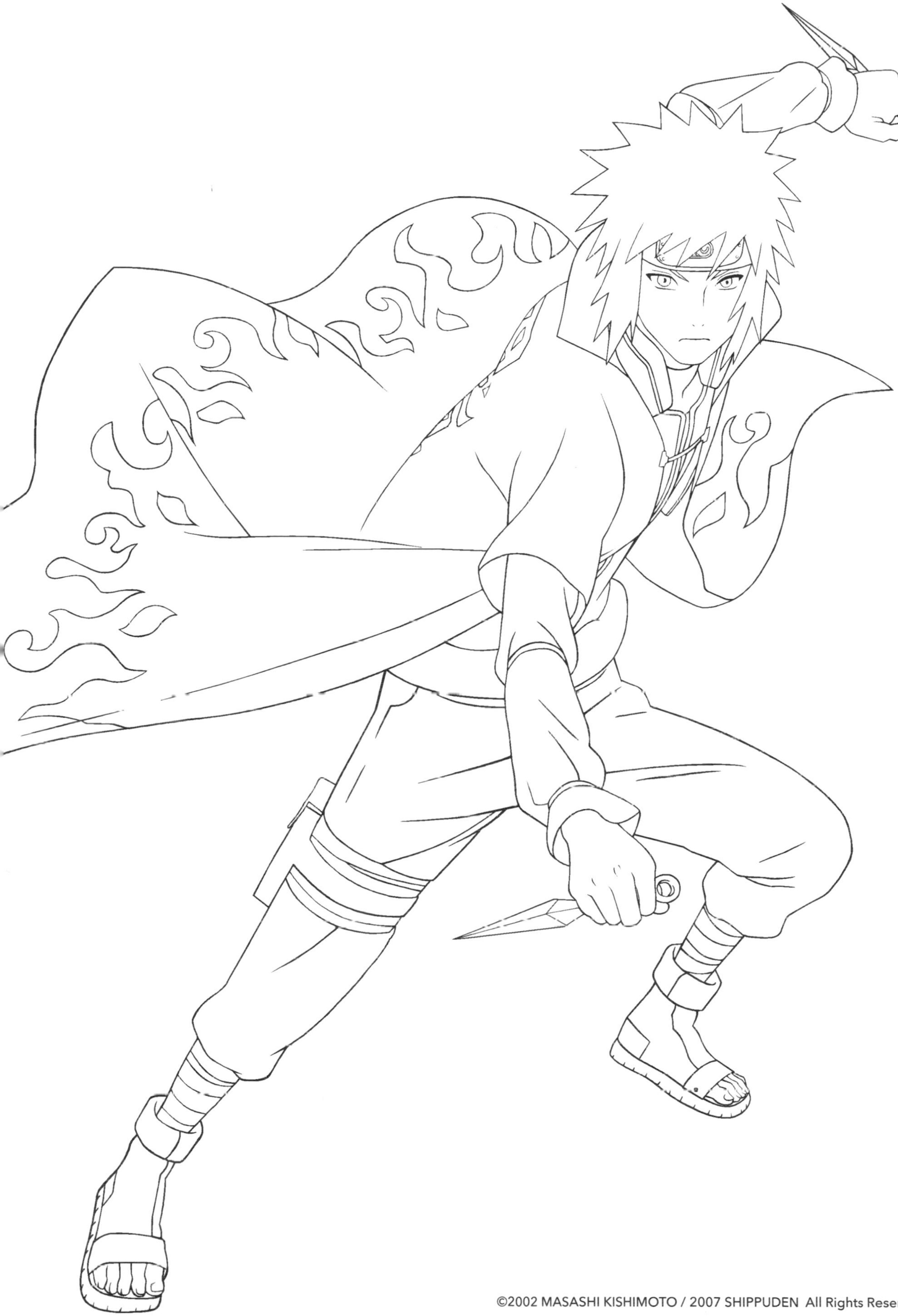

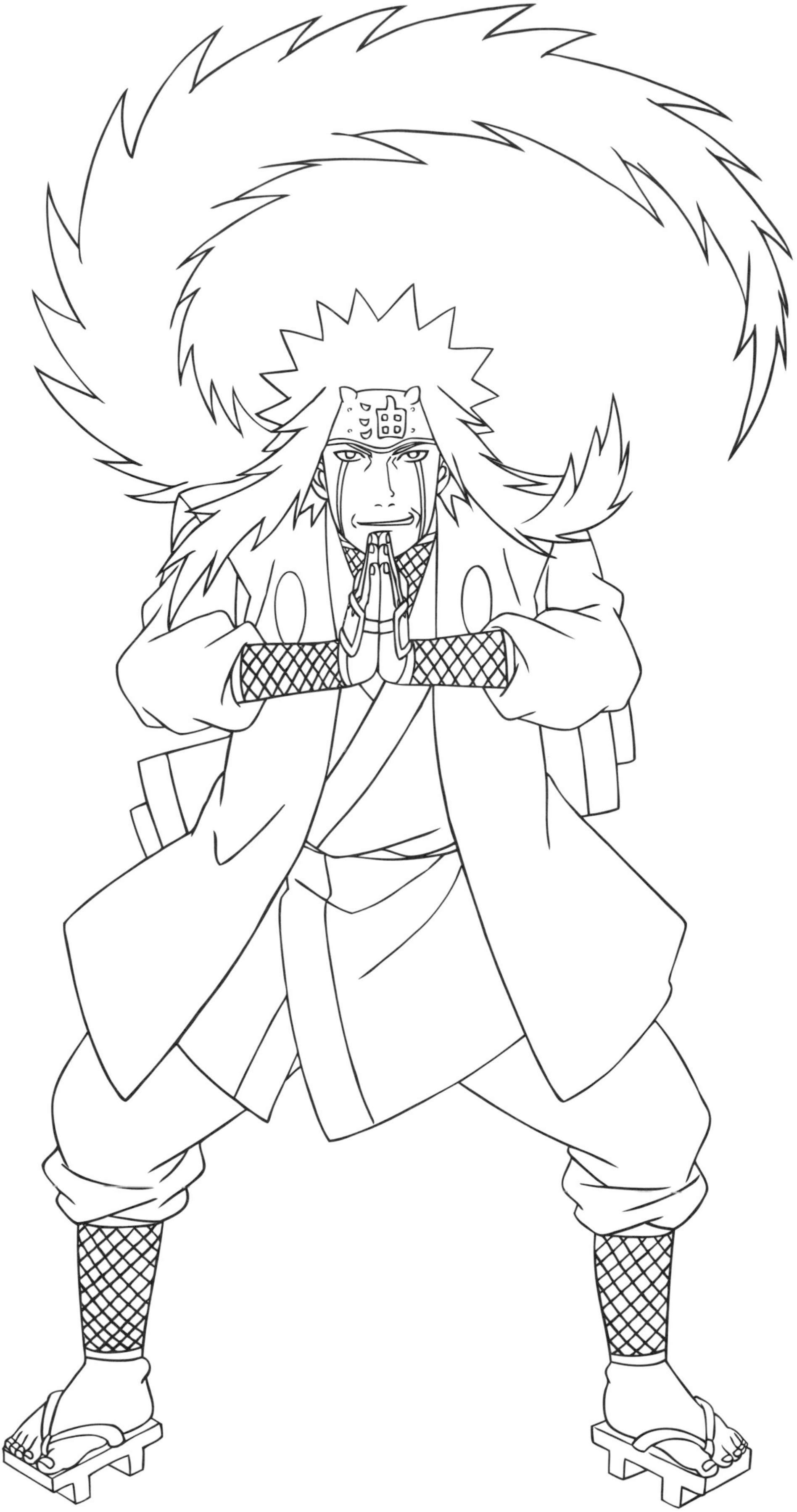

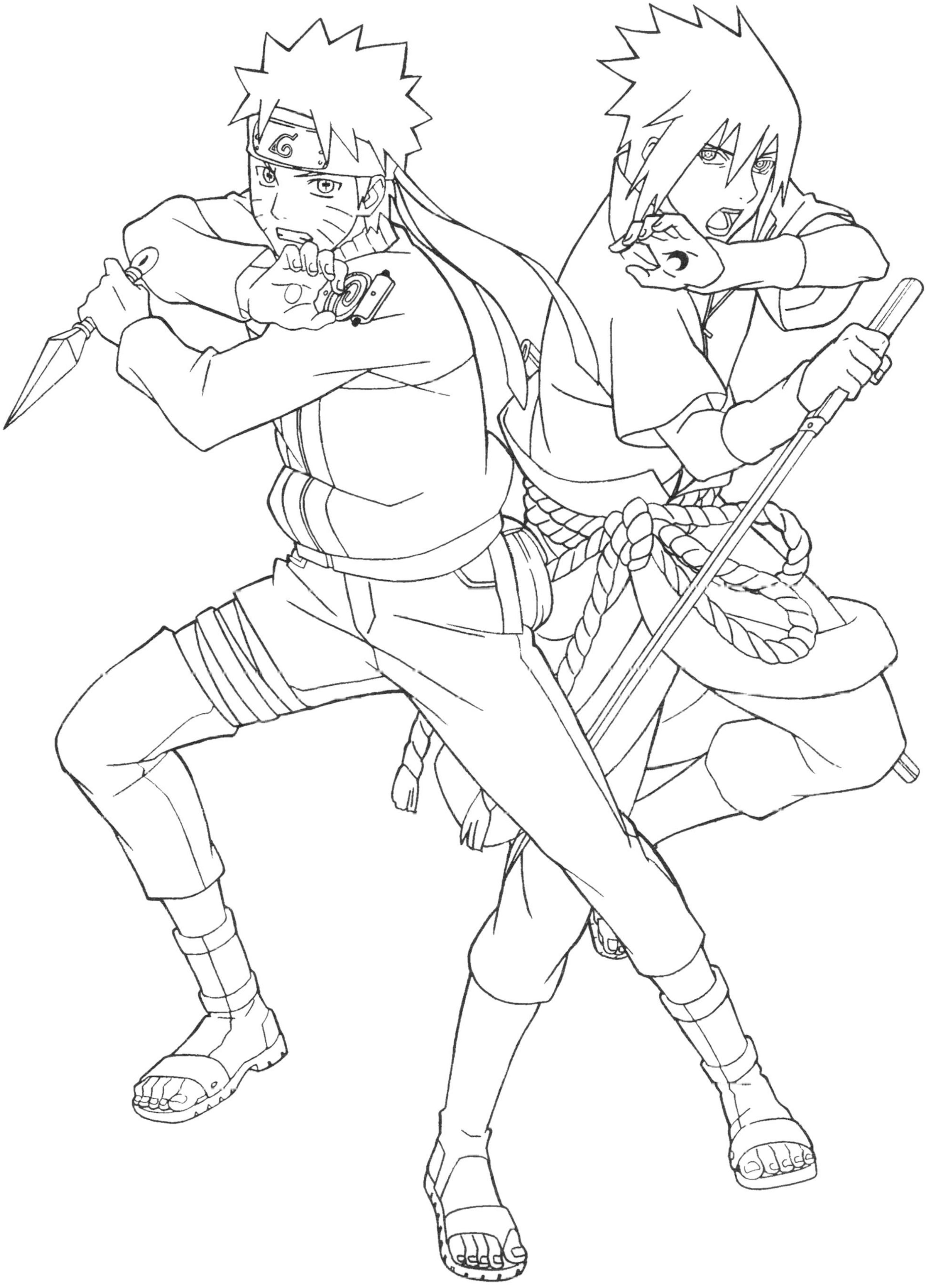

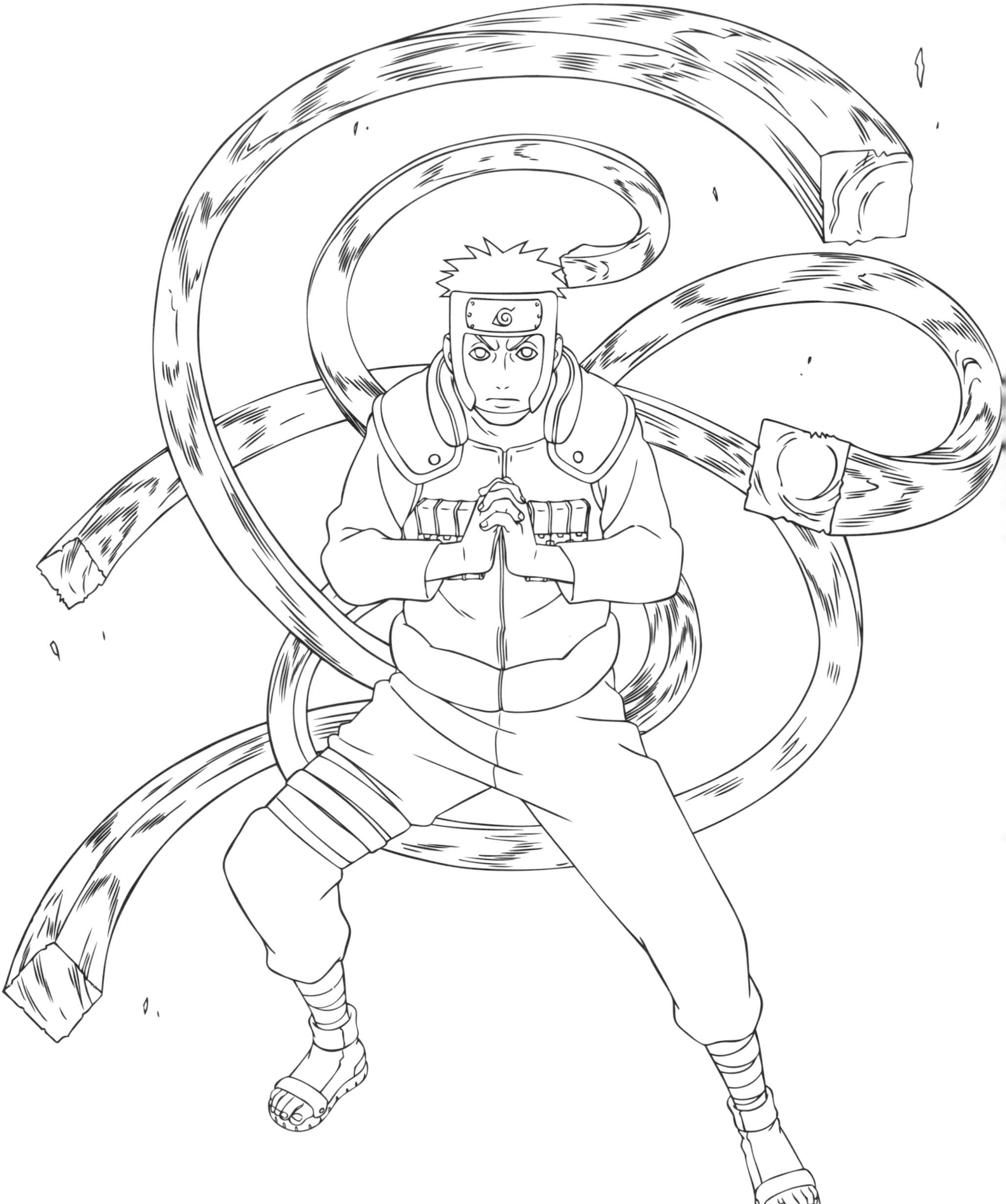

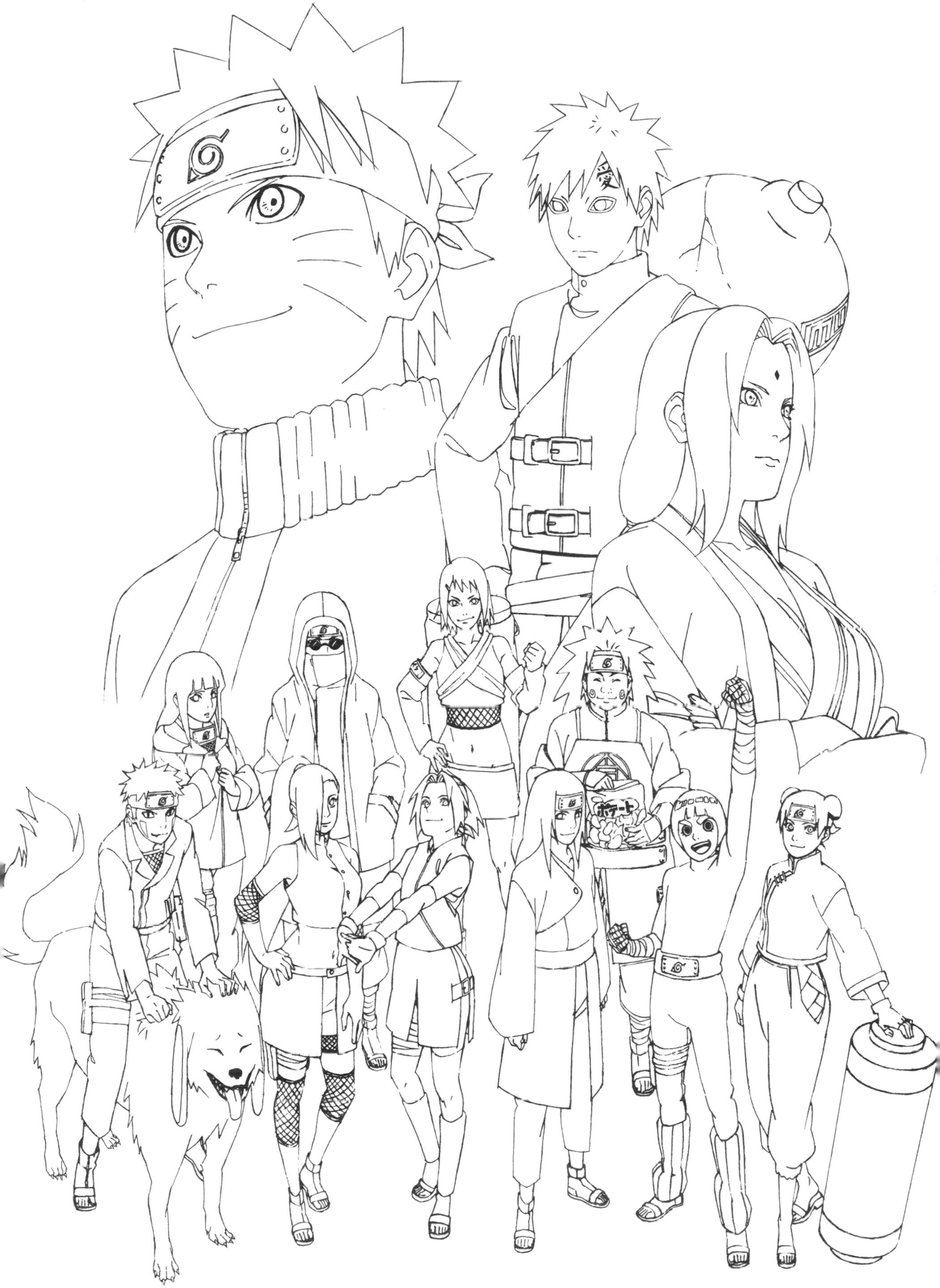
ポテート

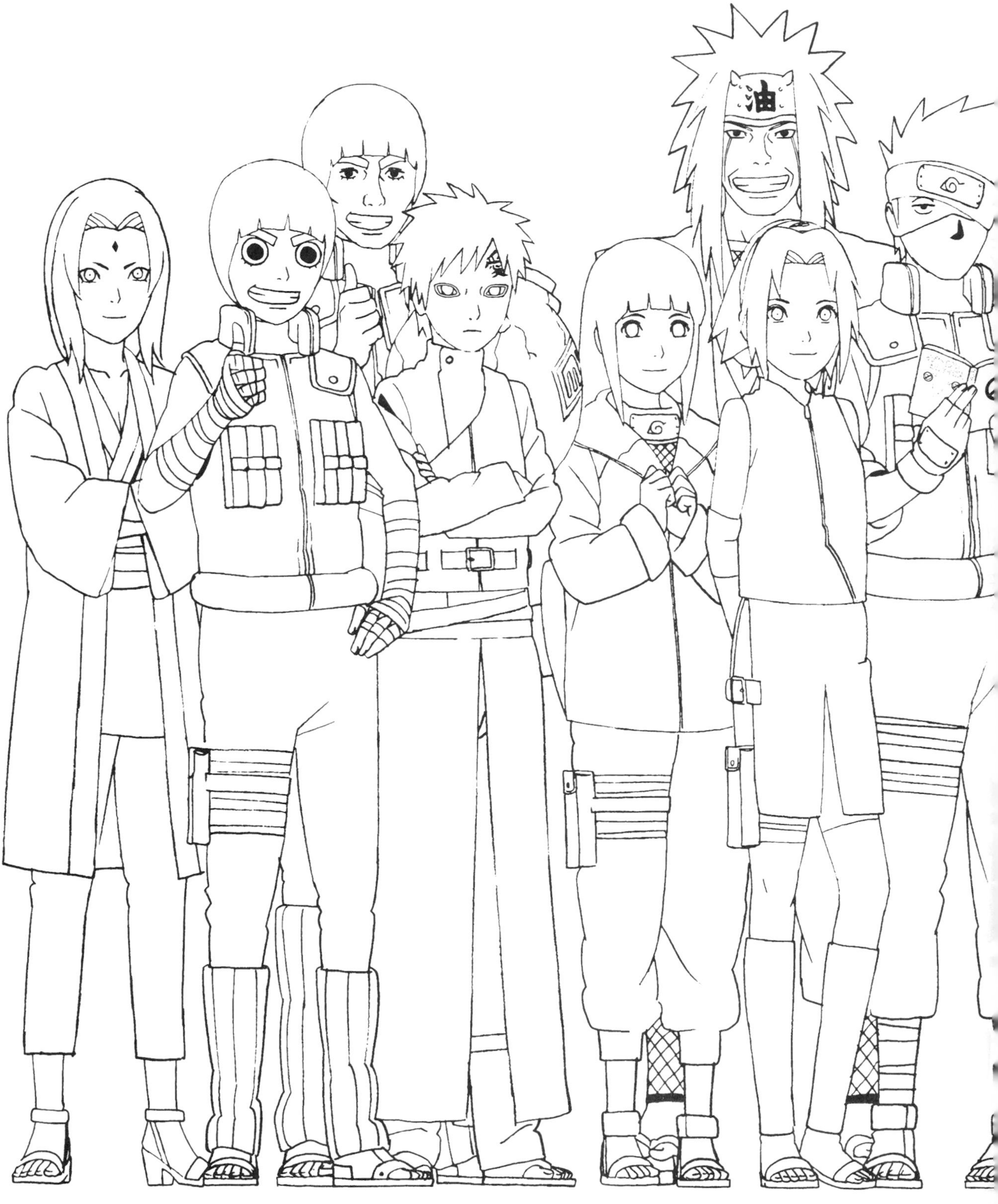

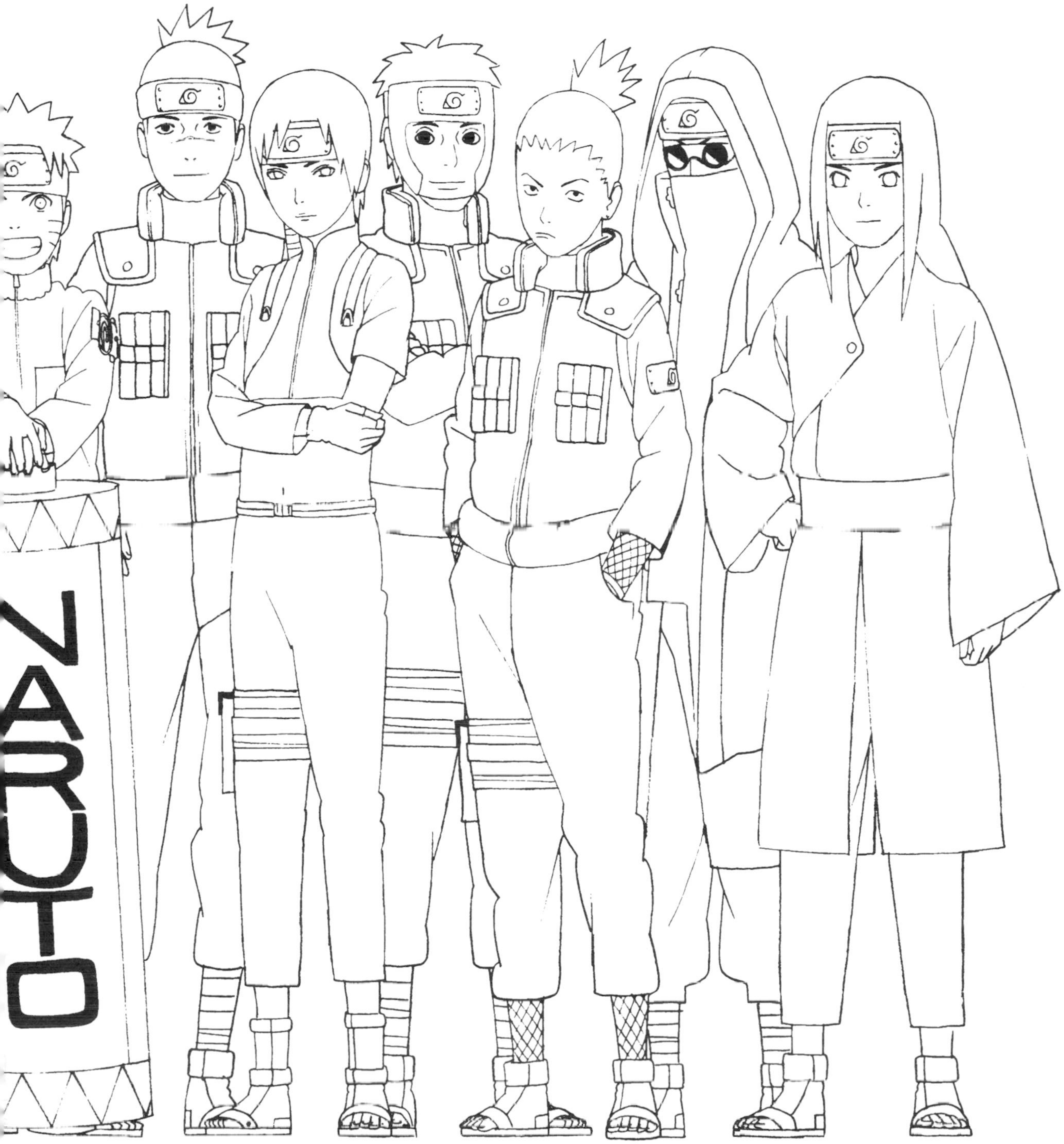
NARUTO

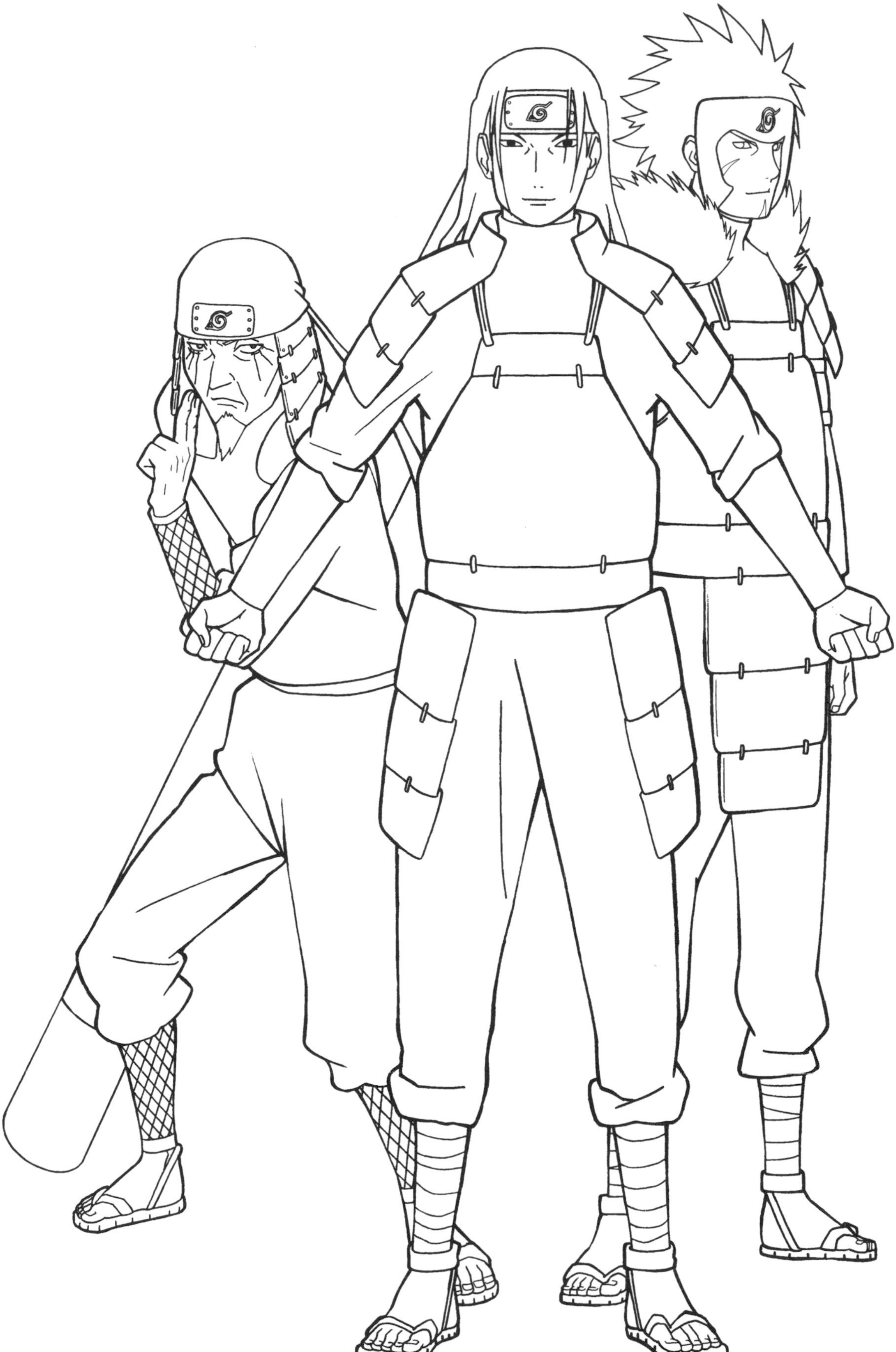

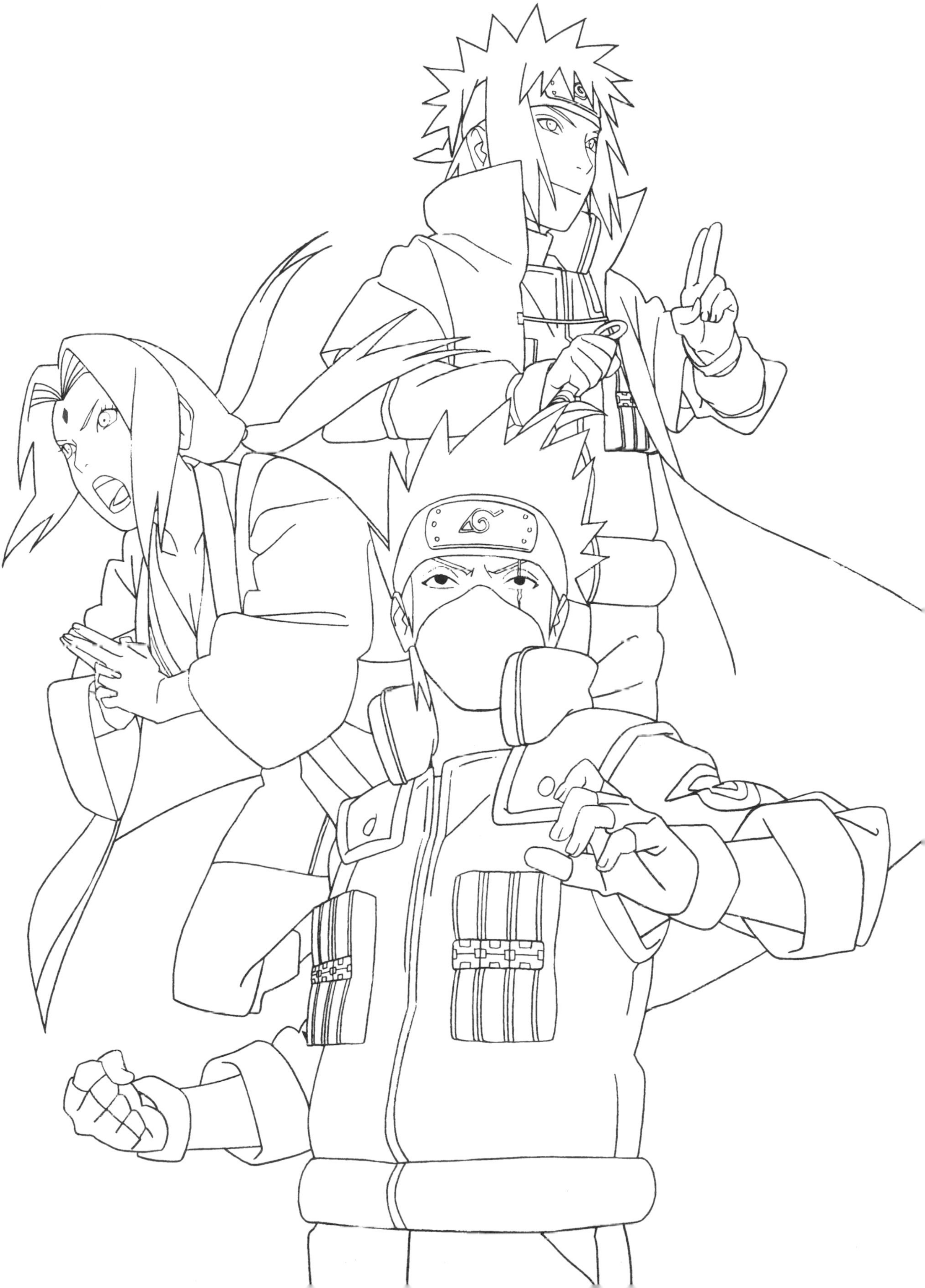

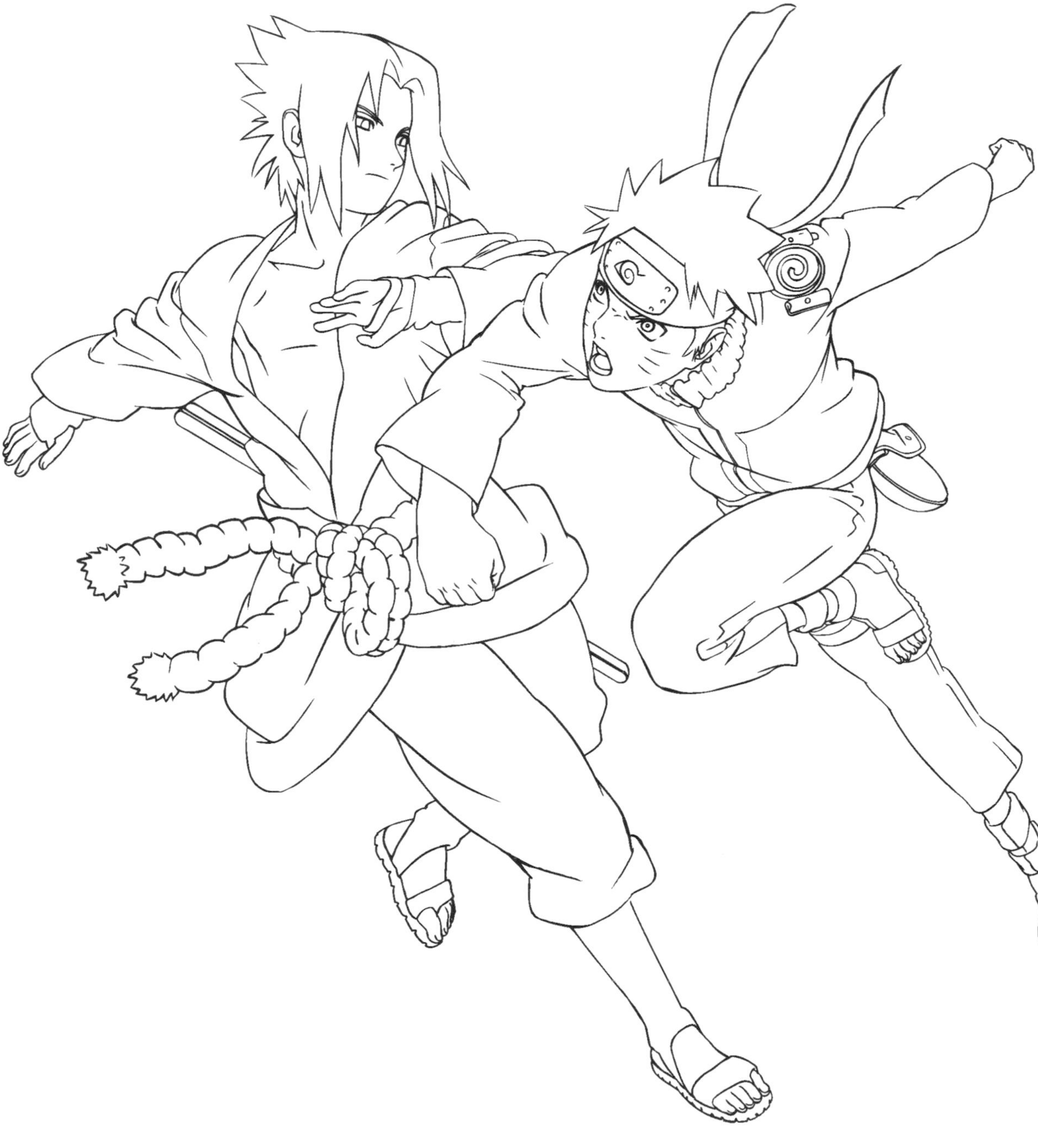

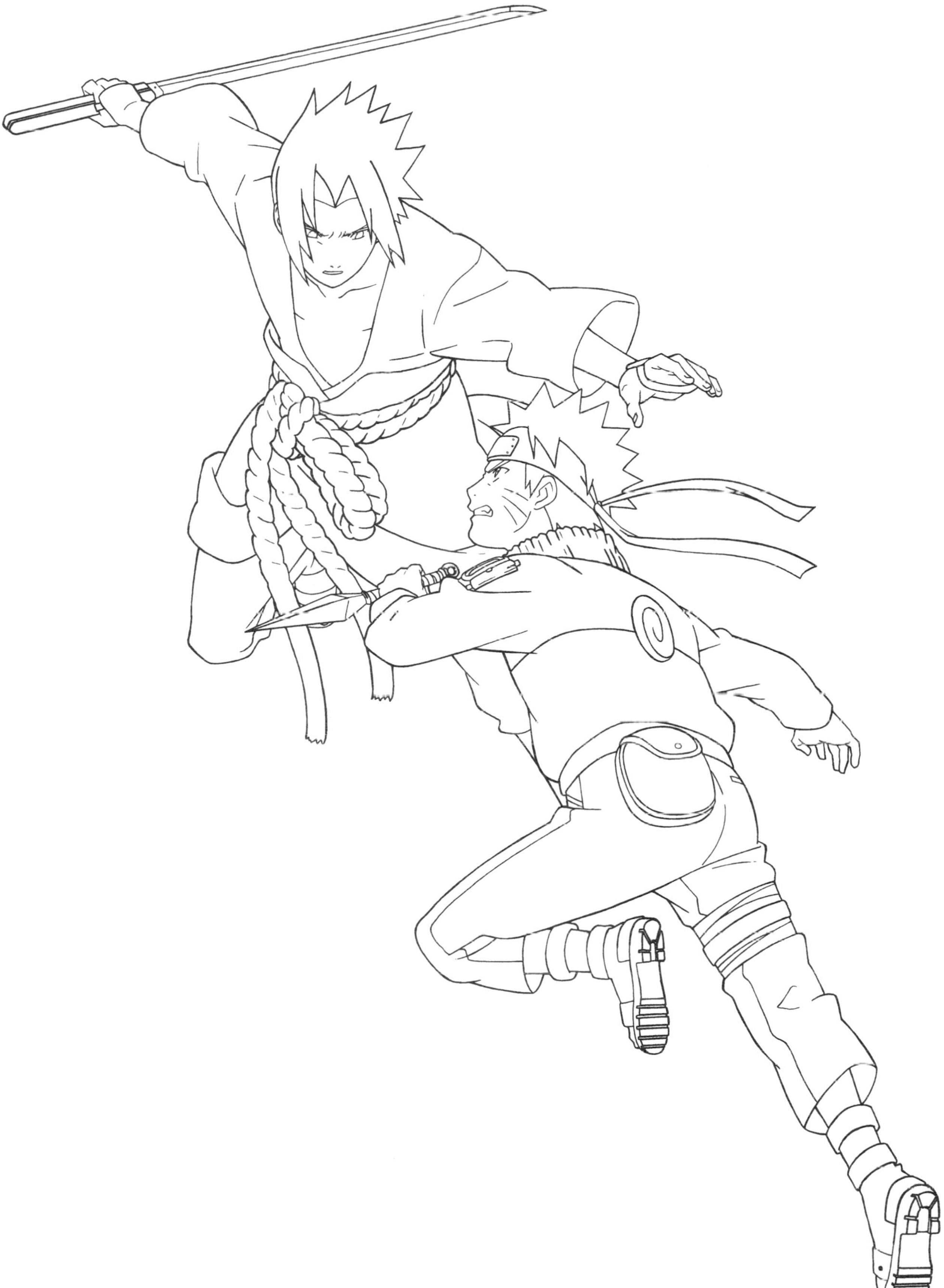

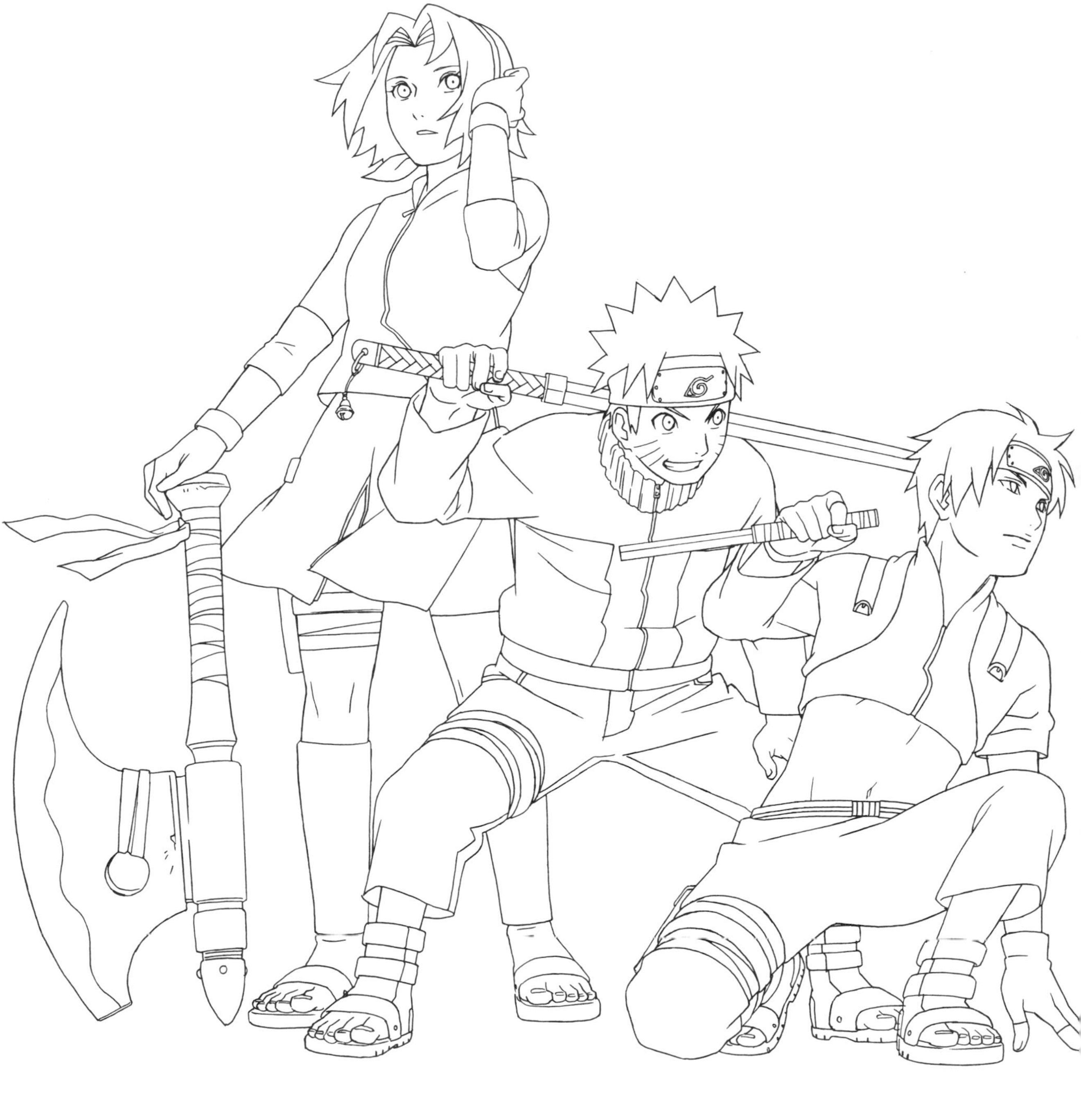

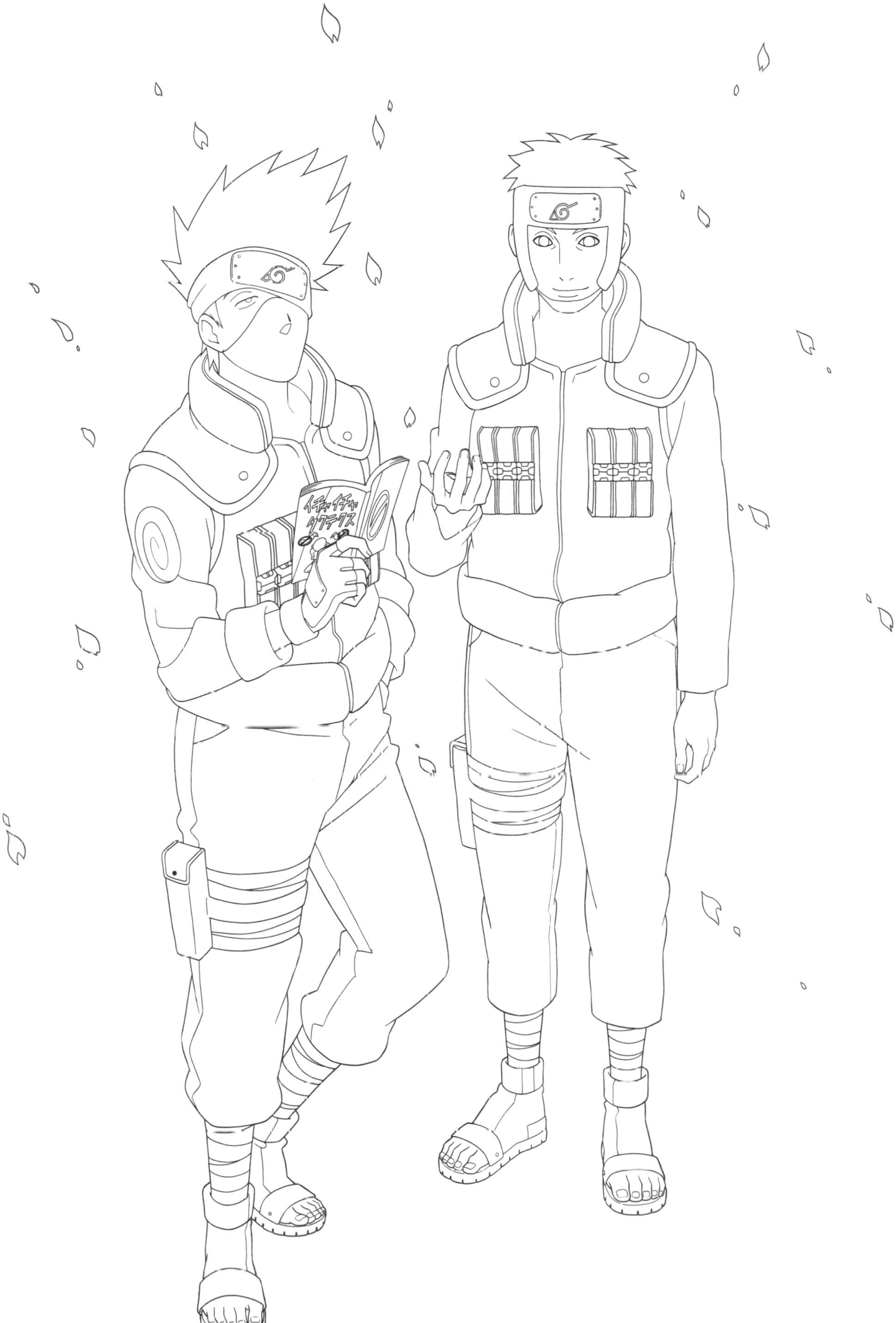
イチャイチャ
タクテクス

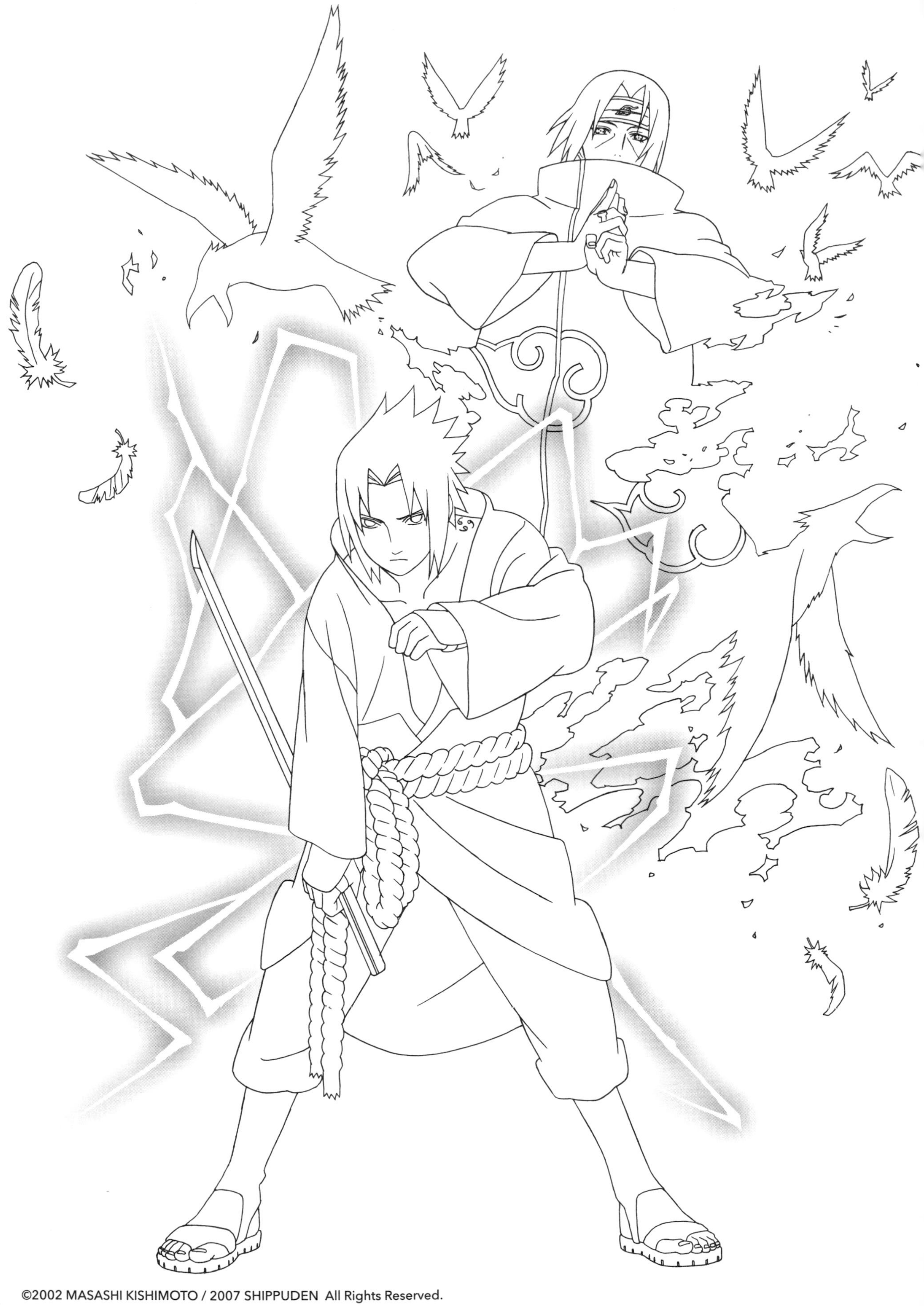

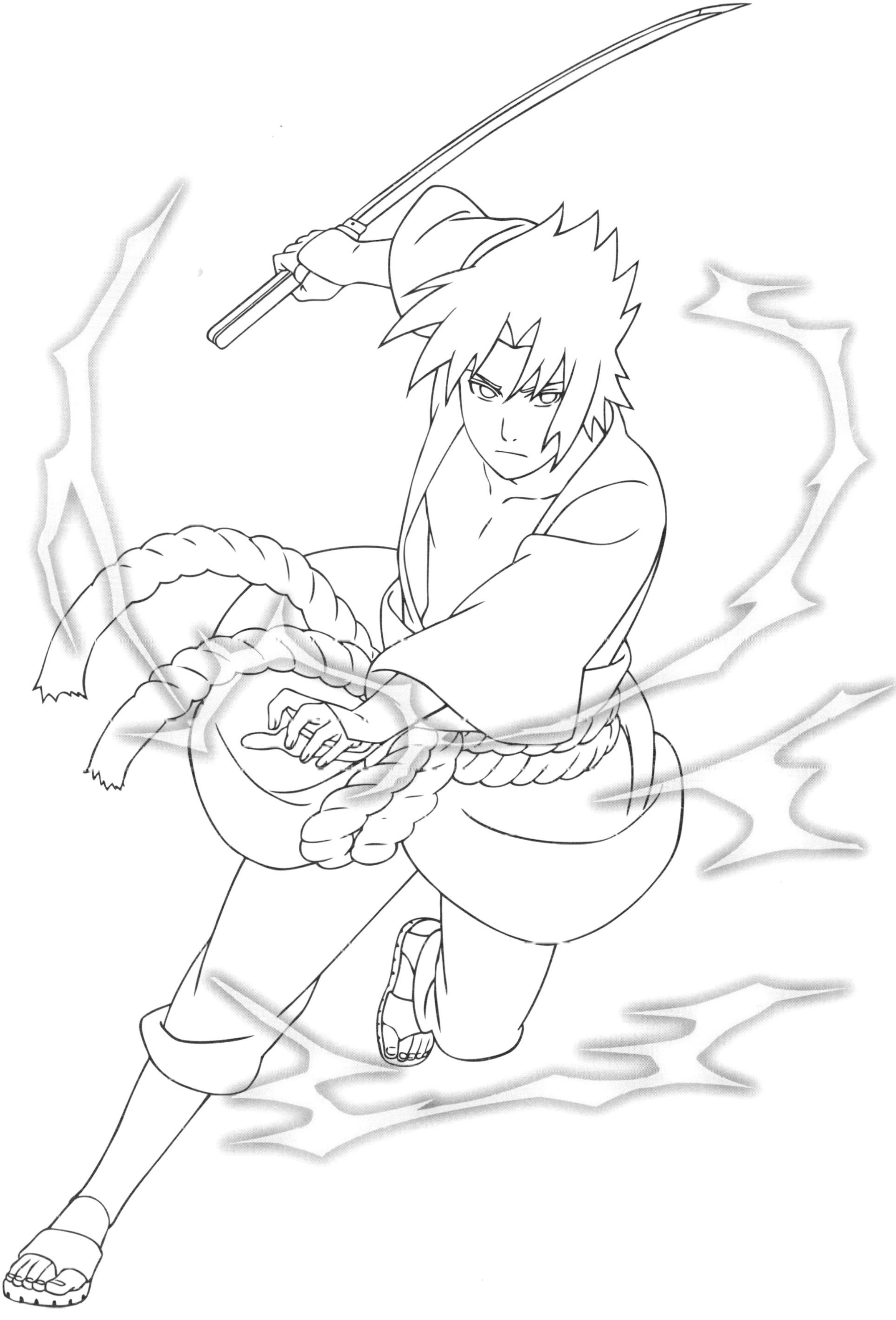

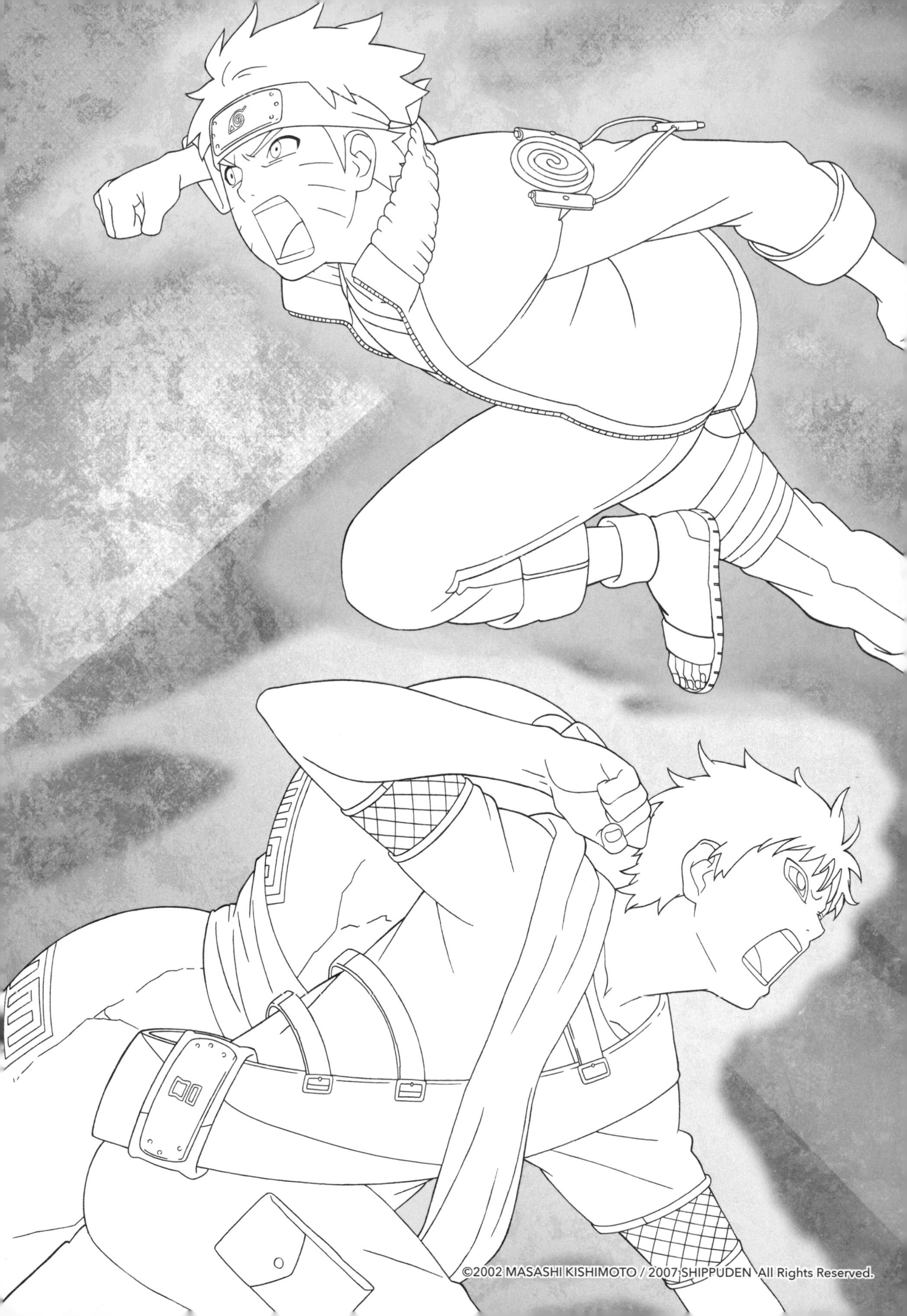

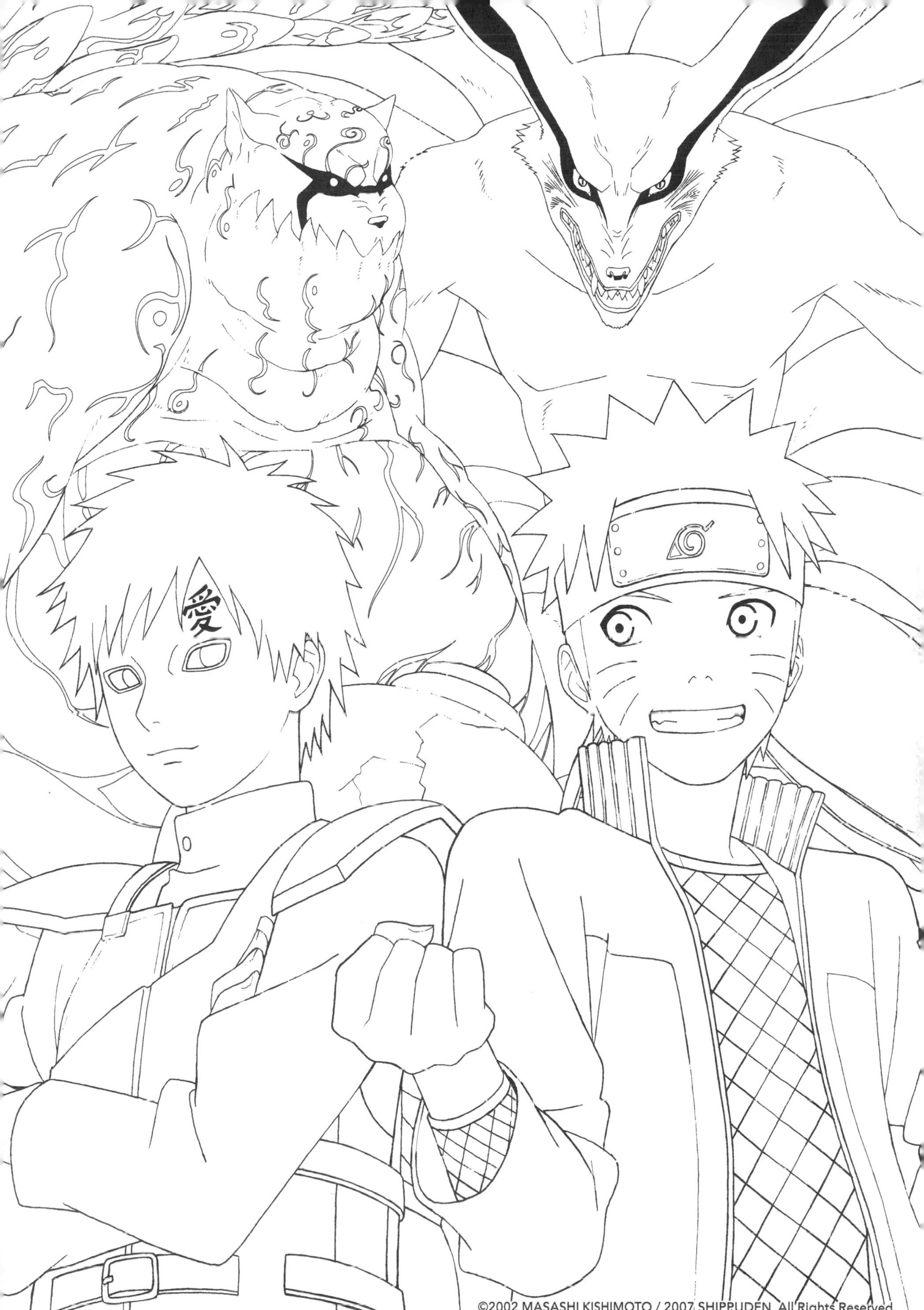
愛

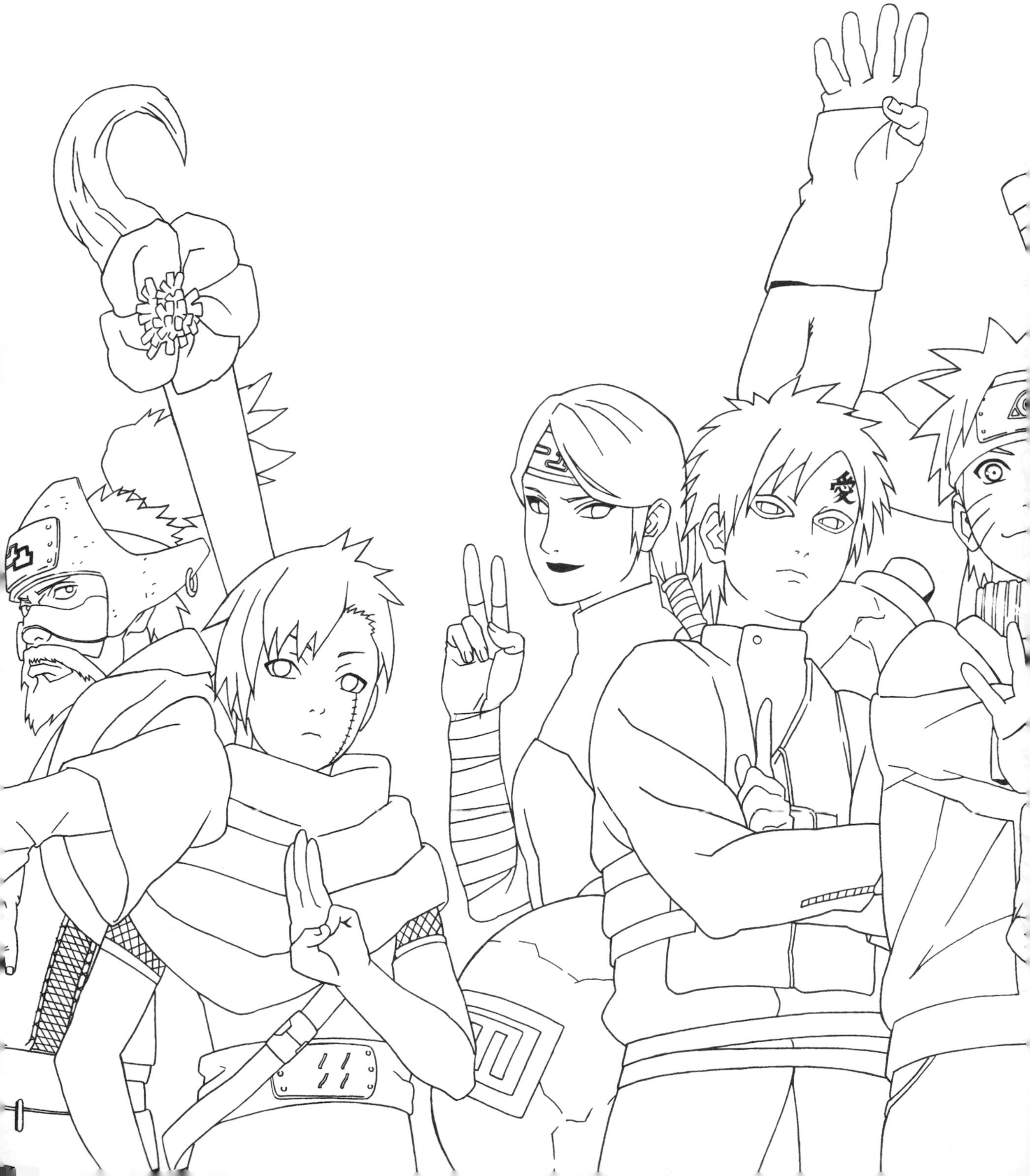
愛

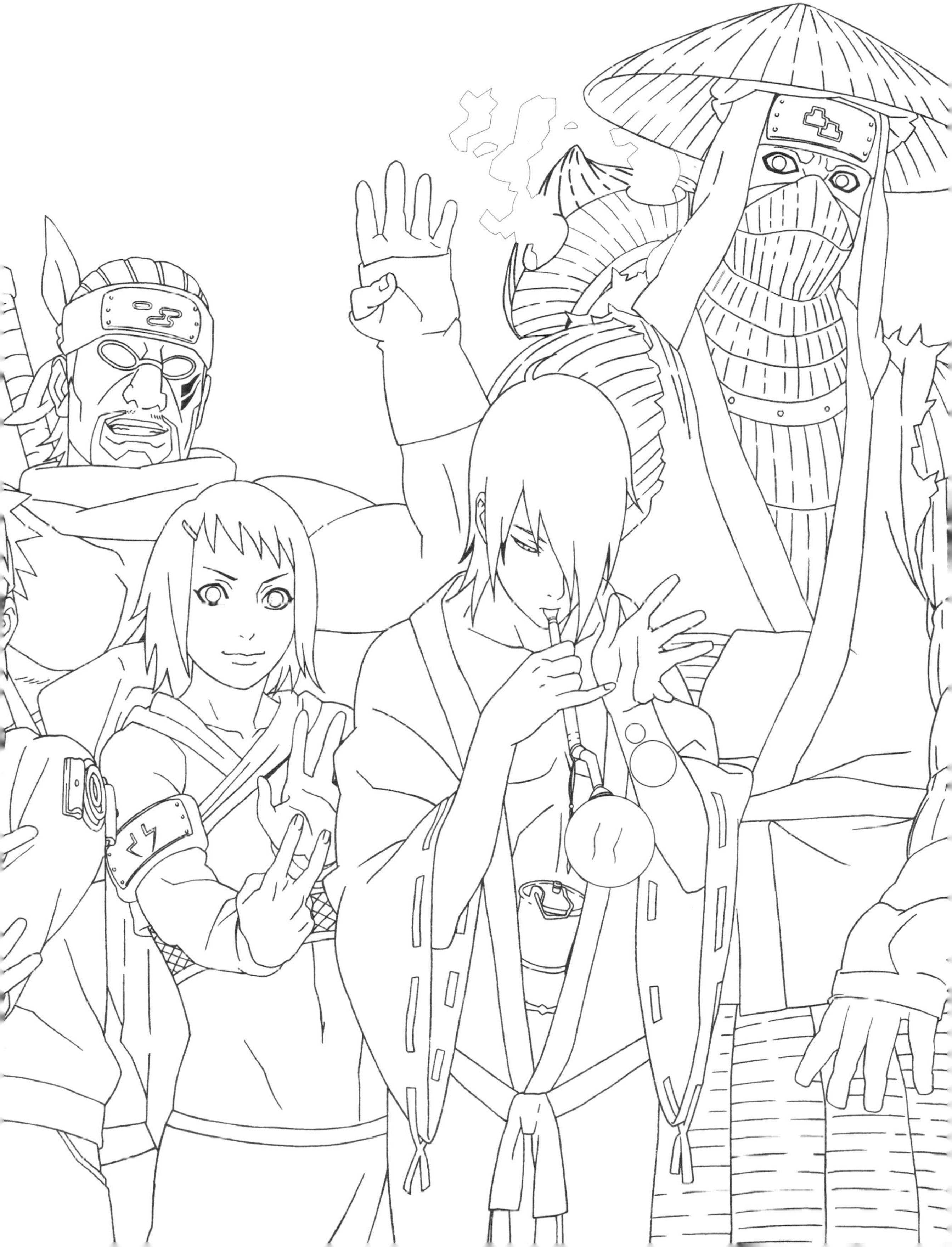

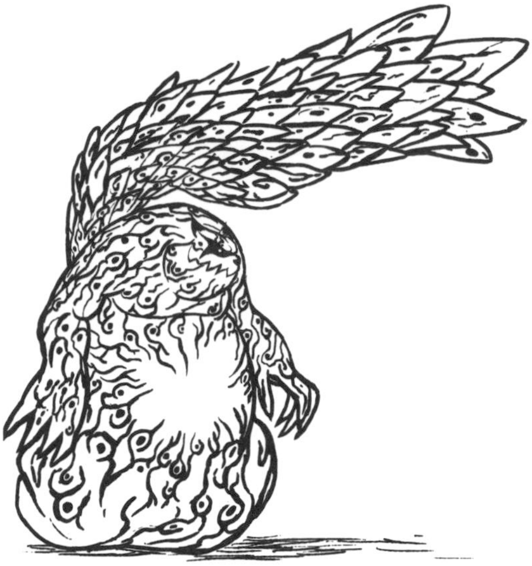

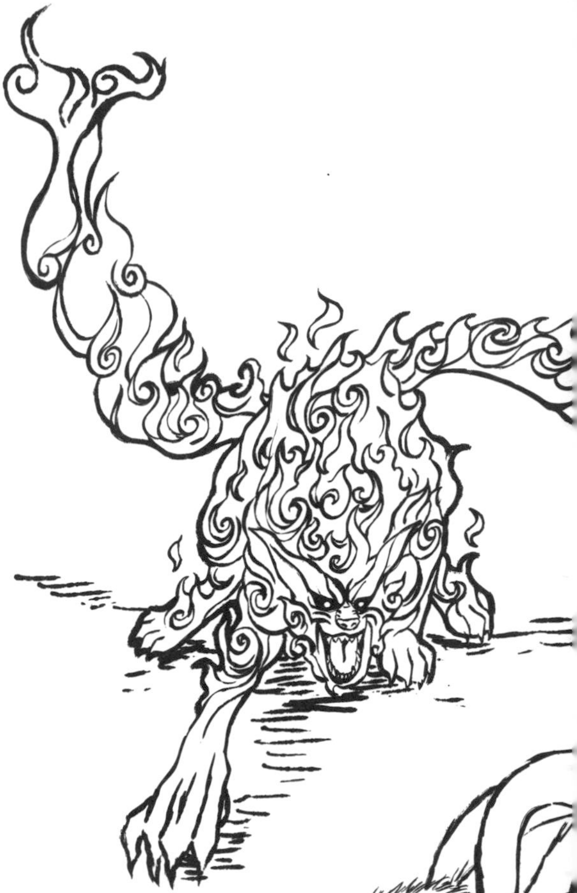

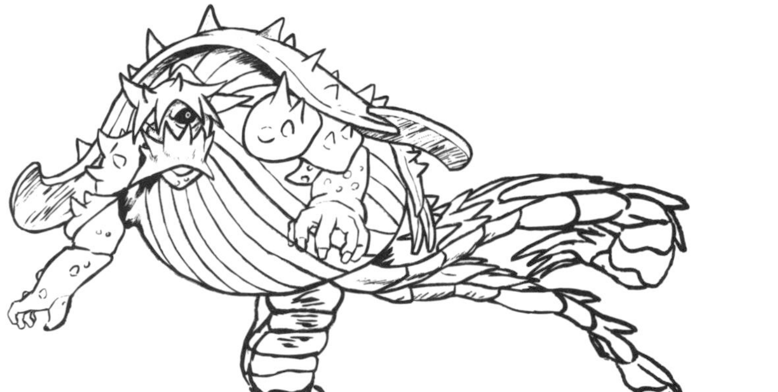

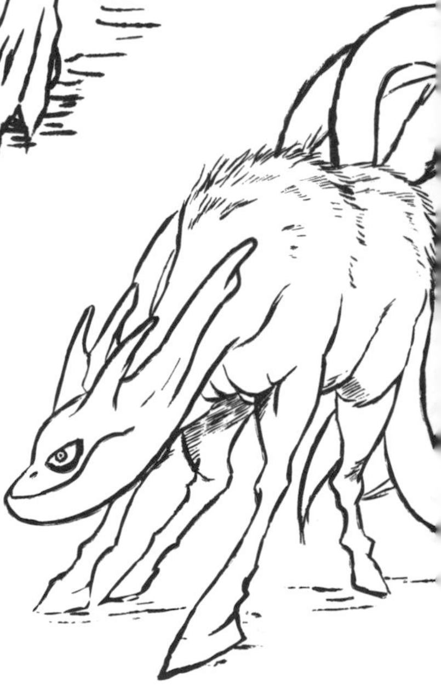

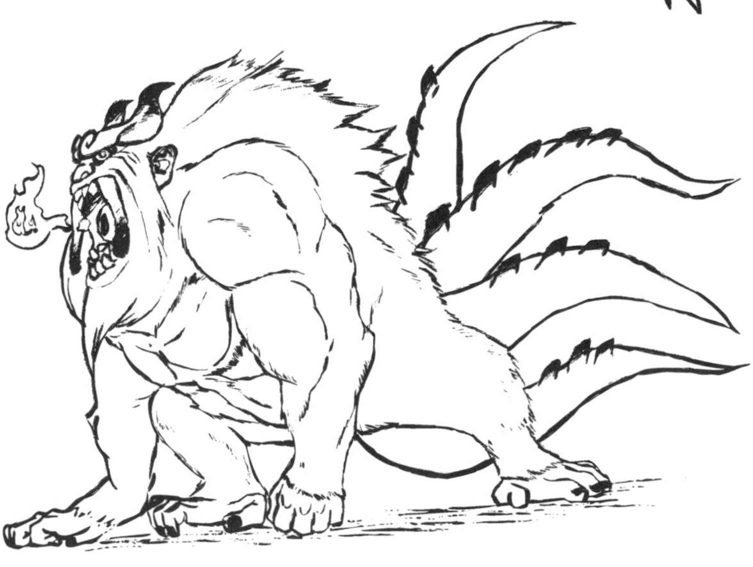

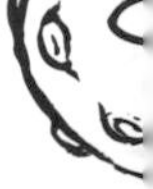

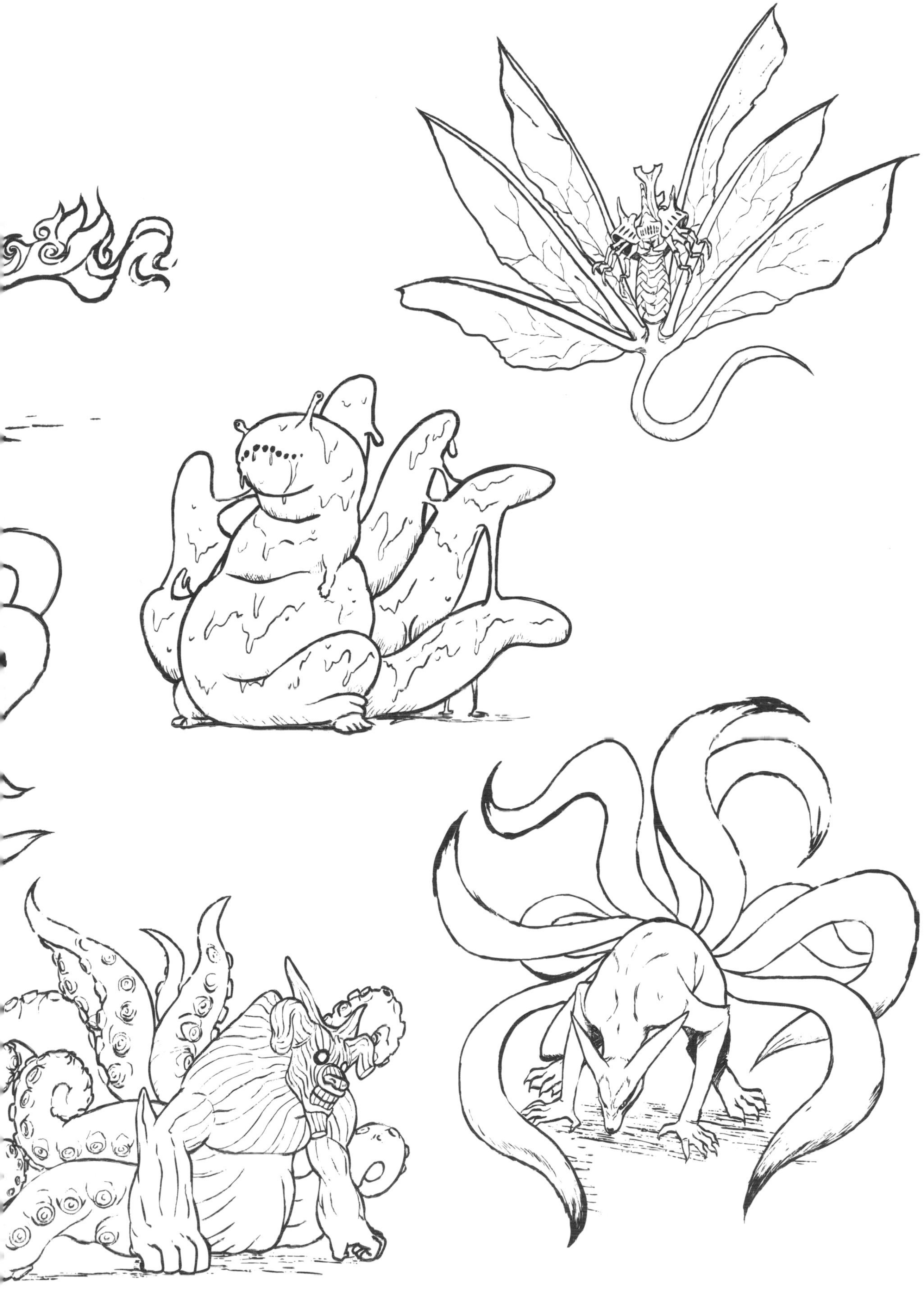

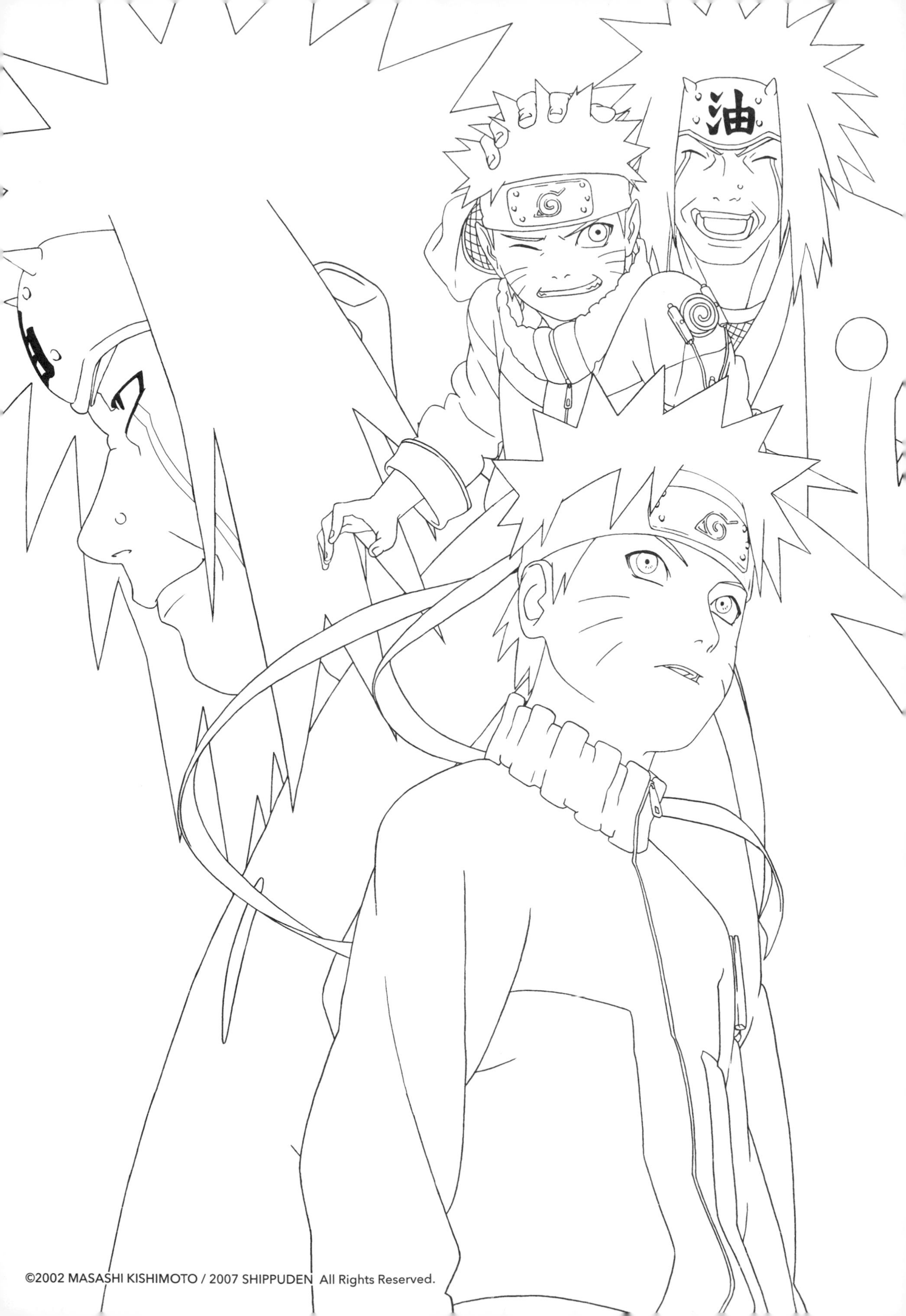
油

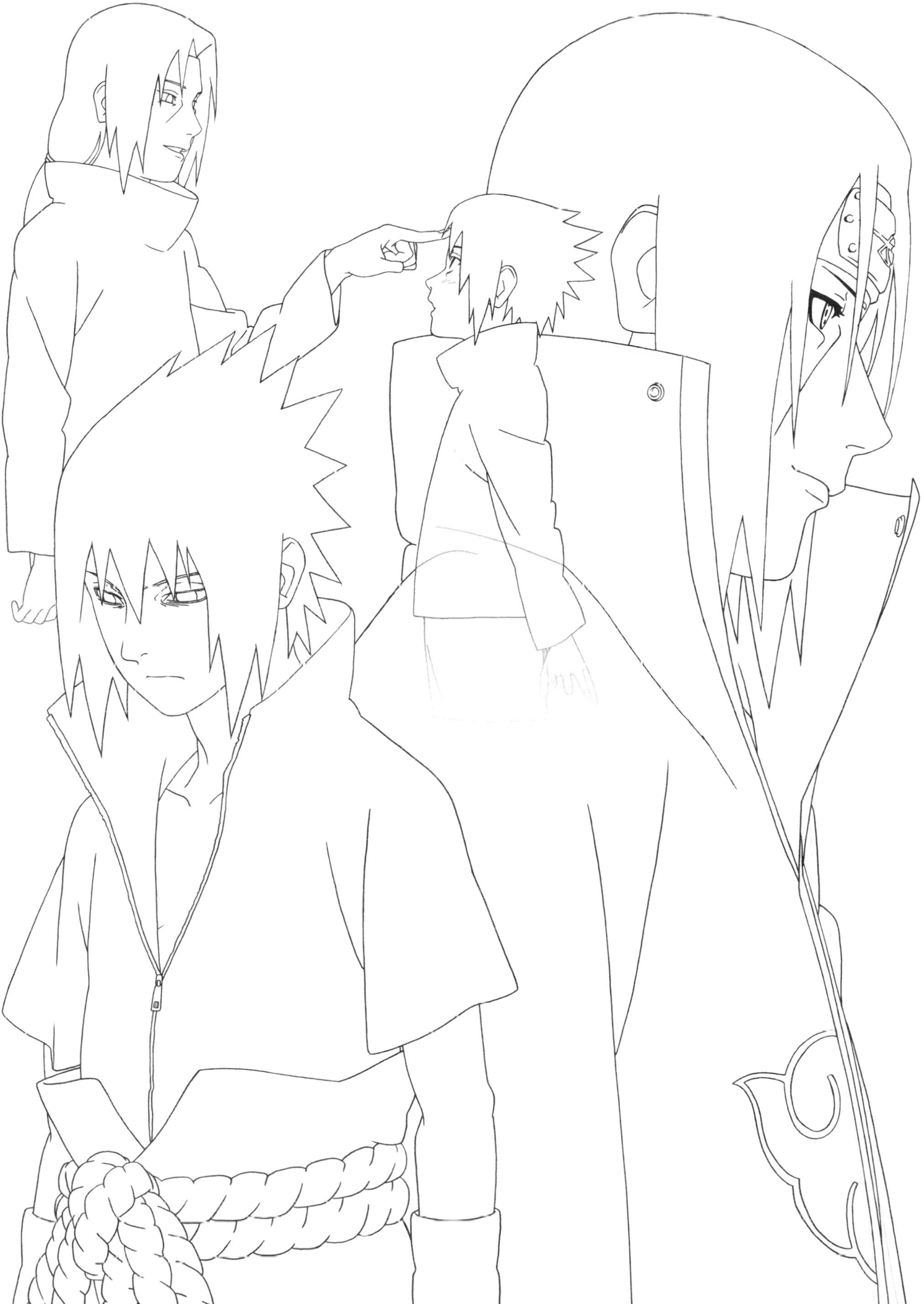

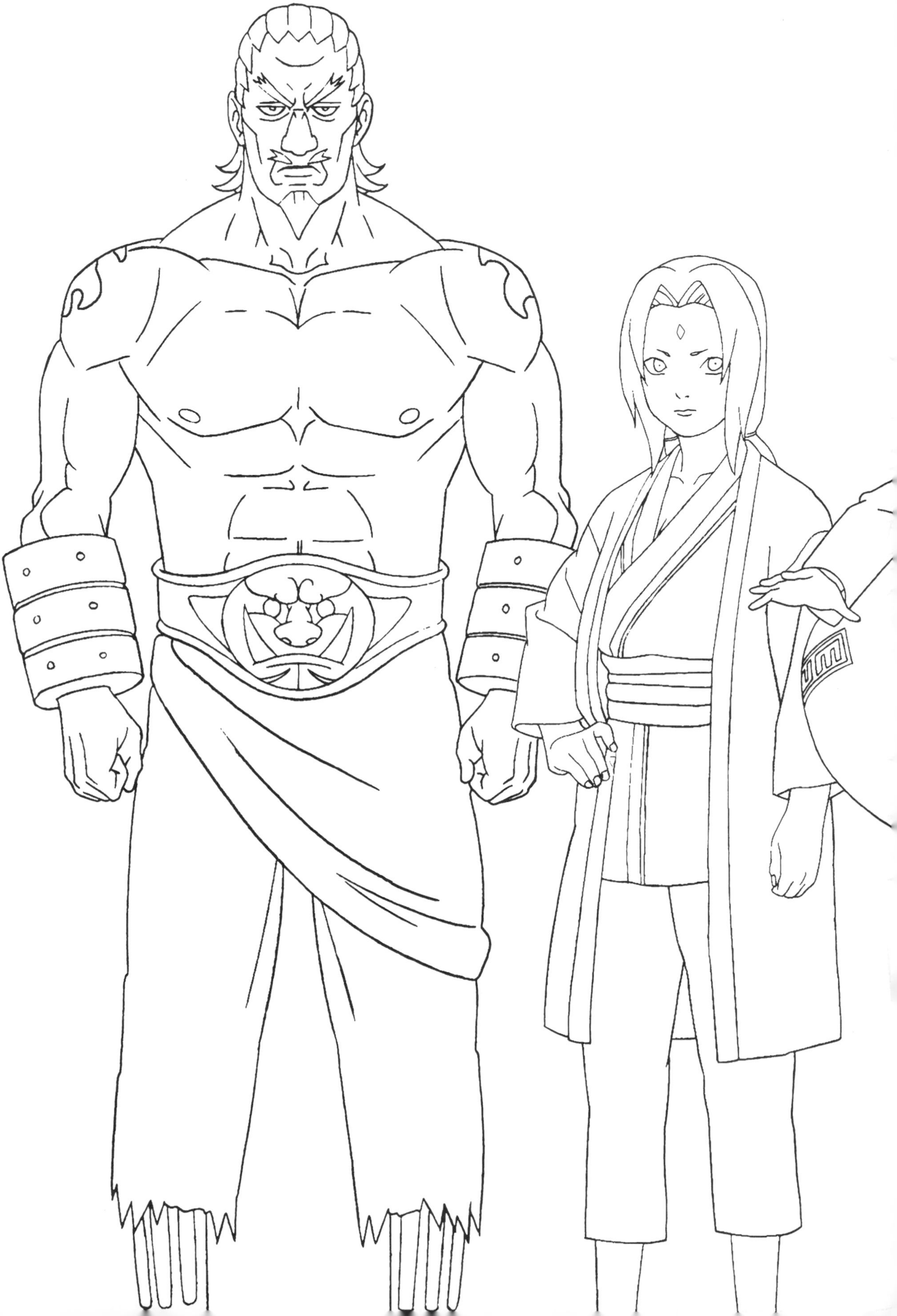

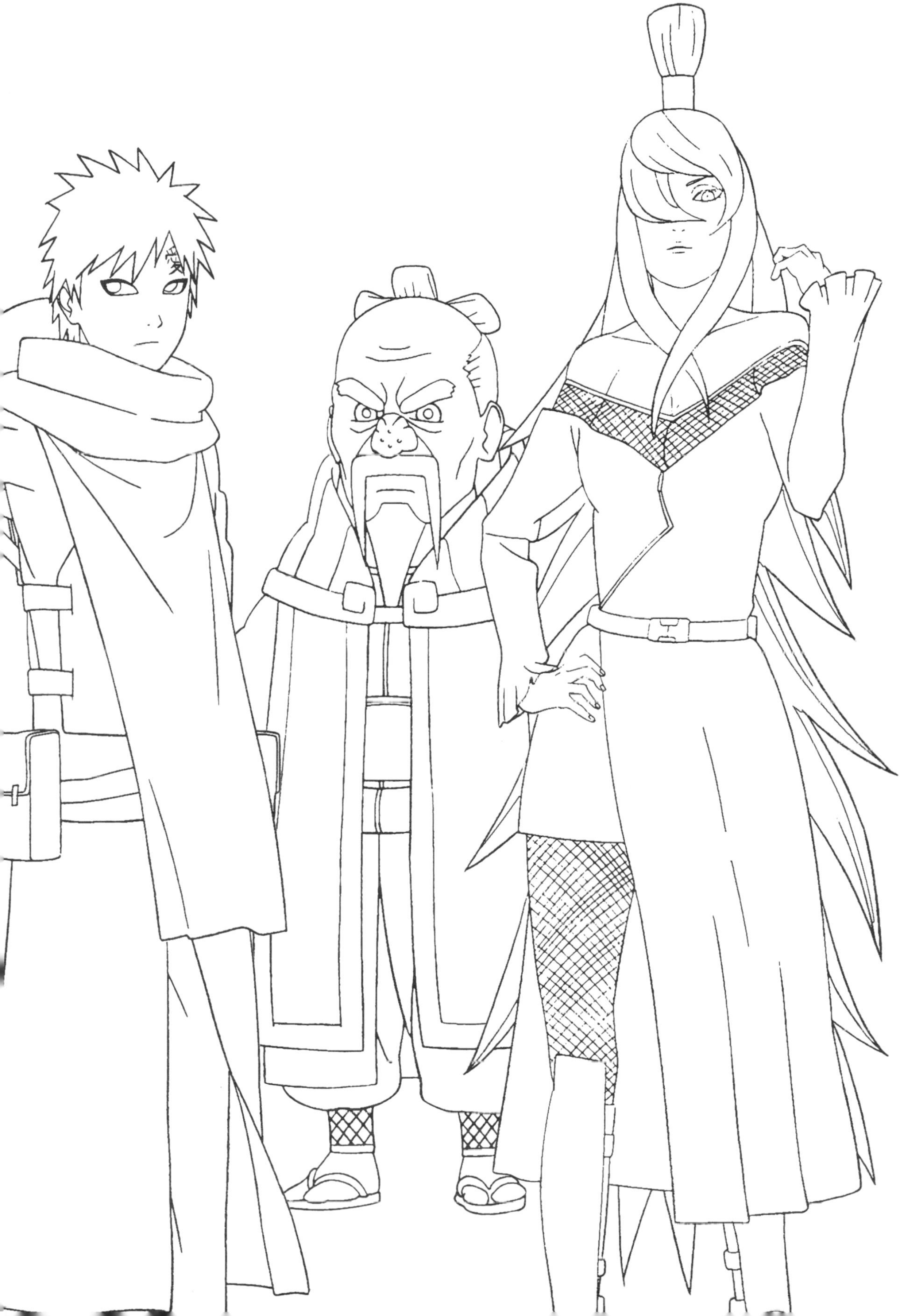

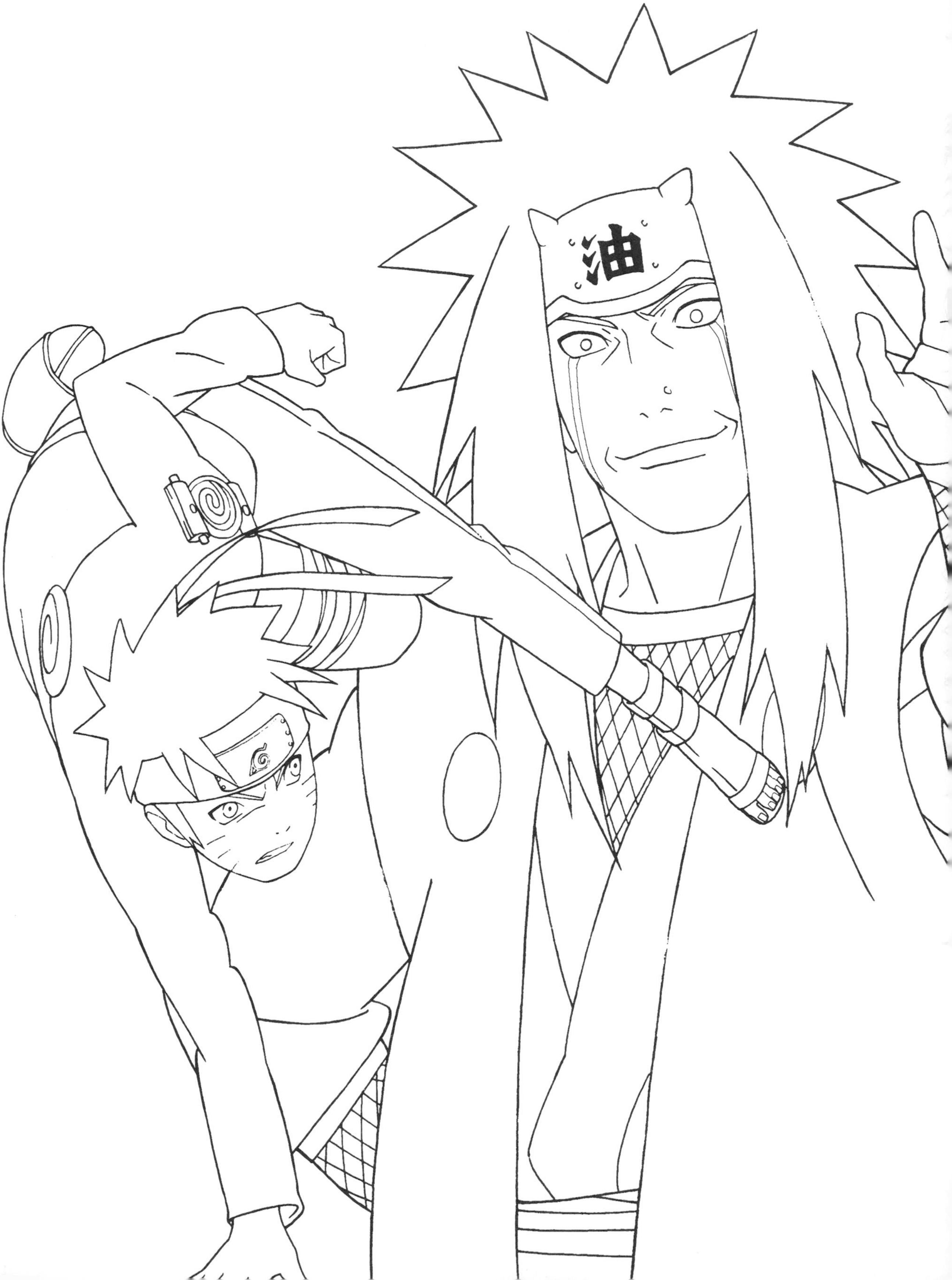
油

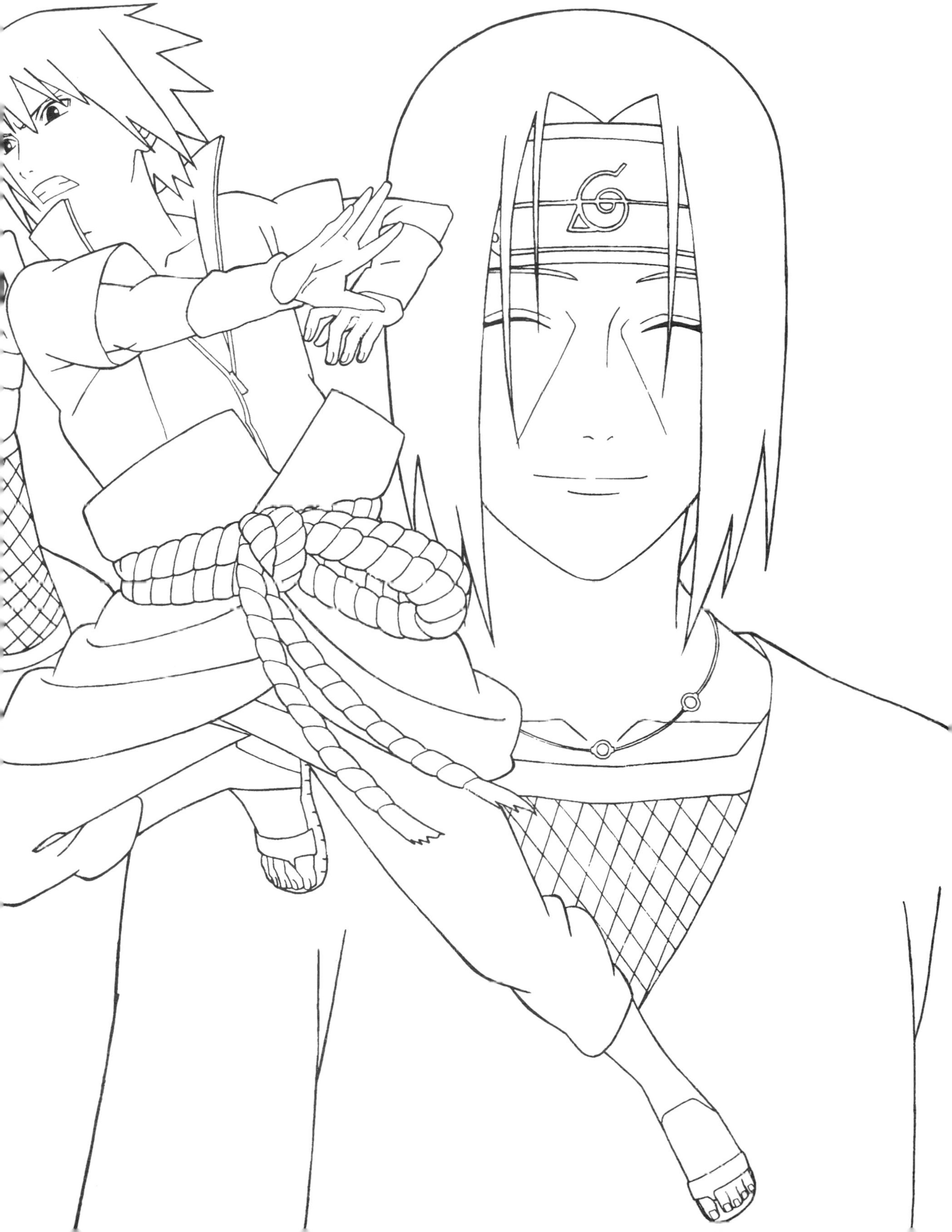

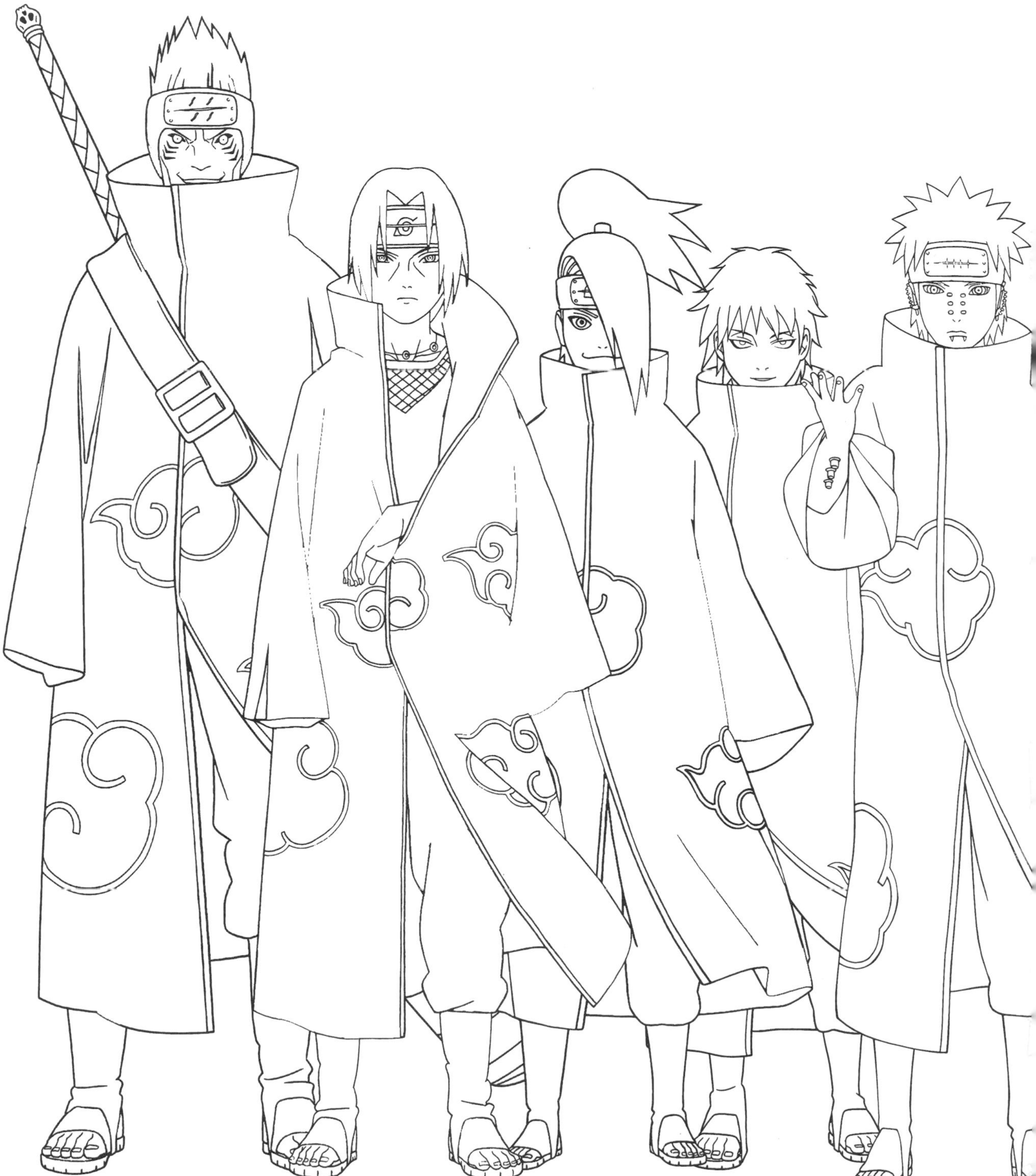

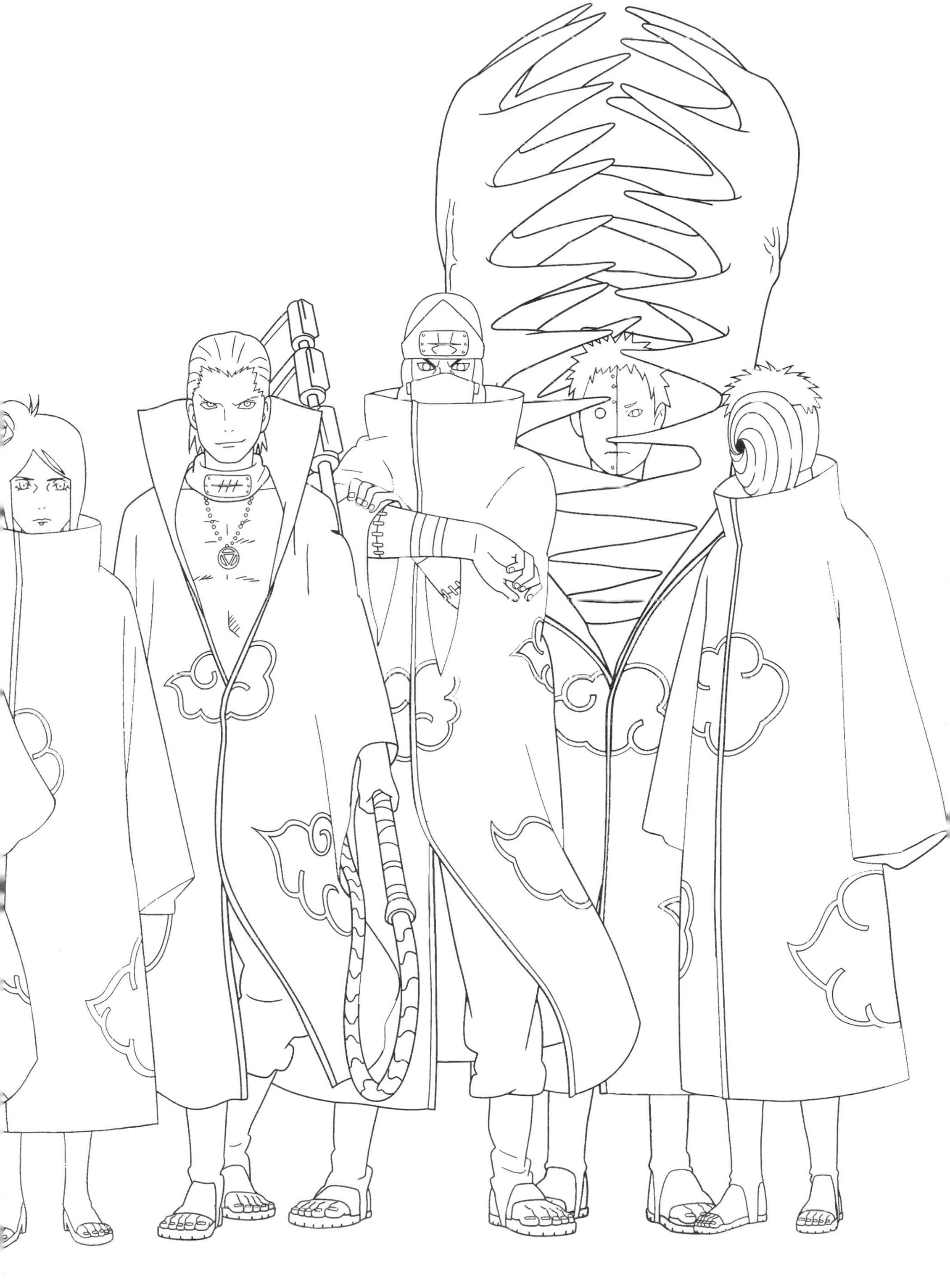

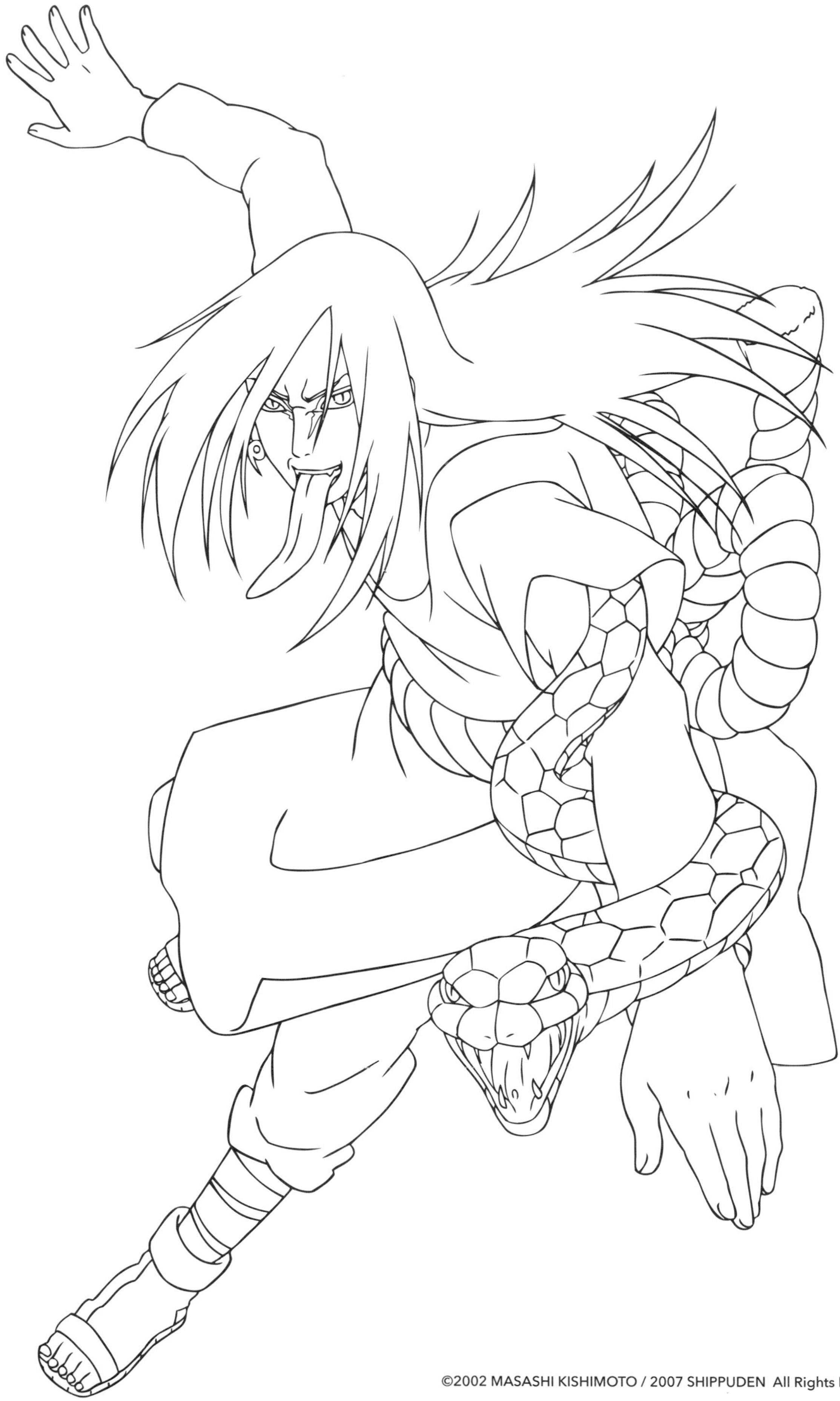

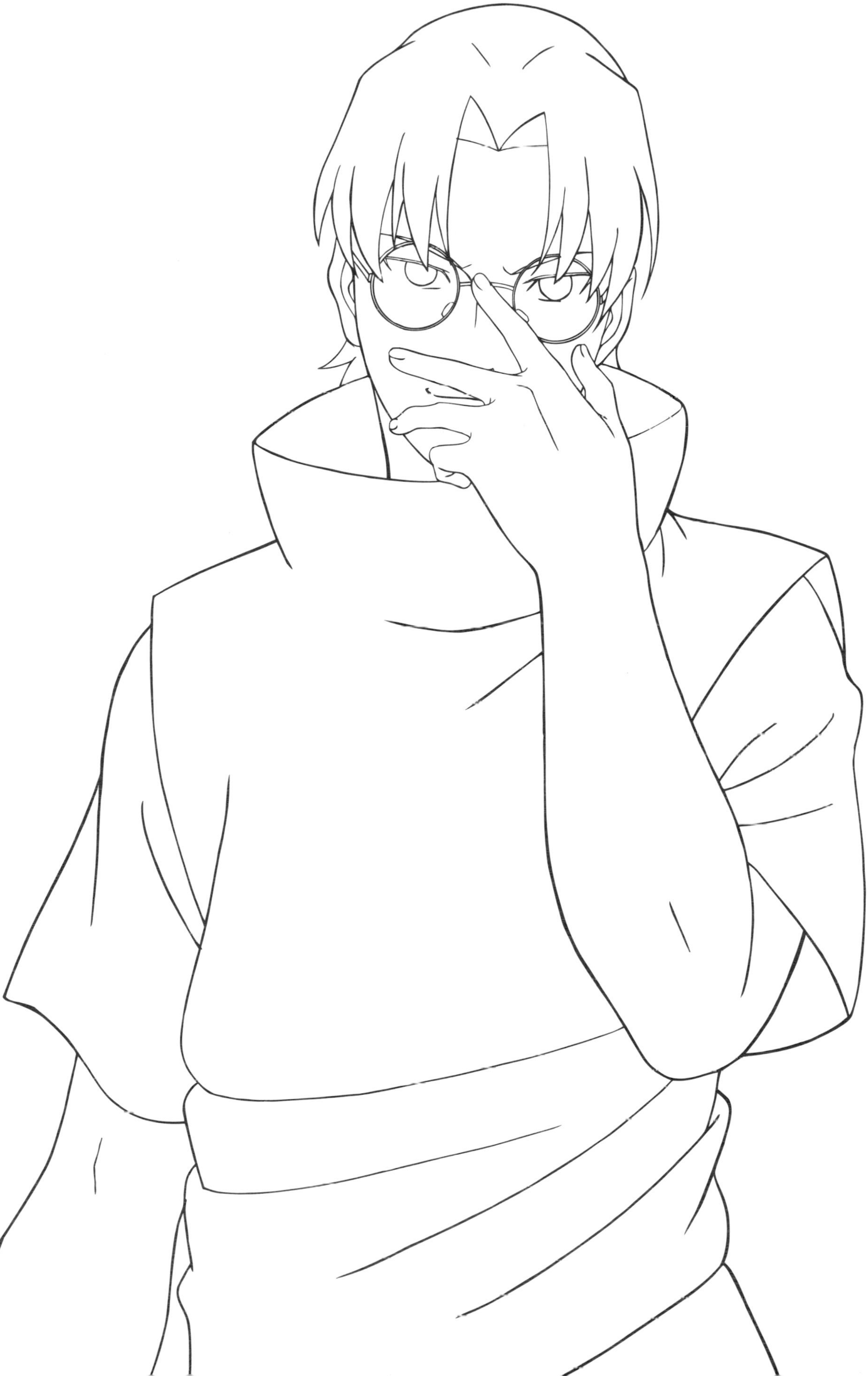

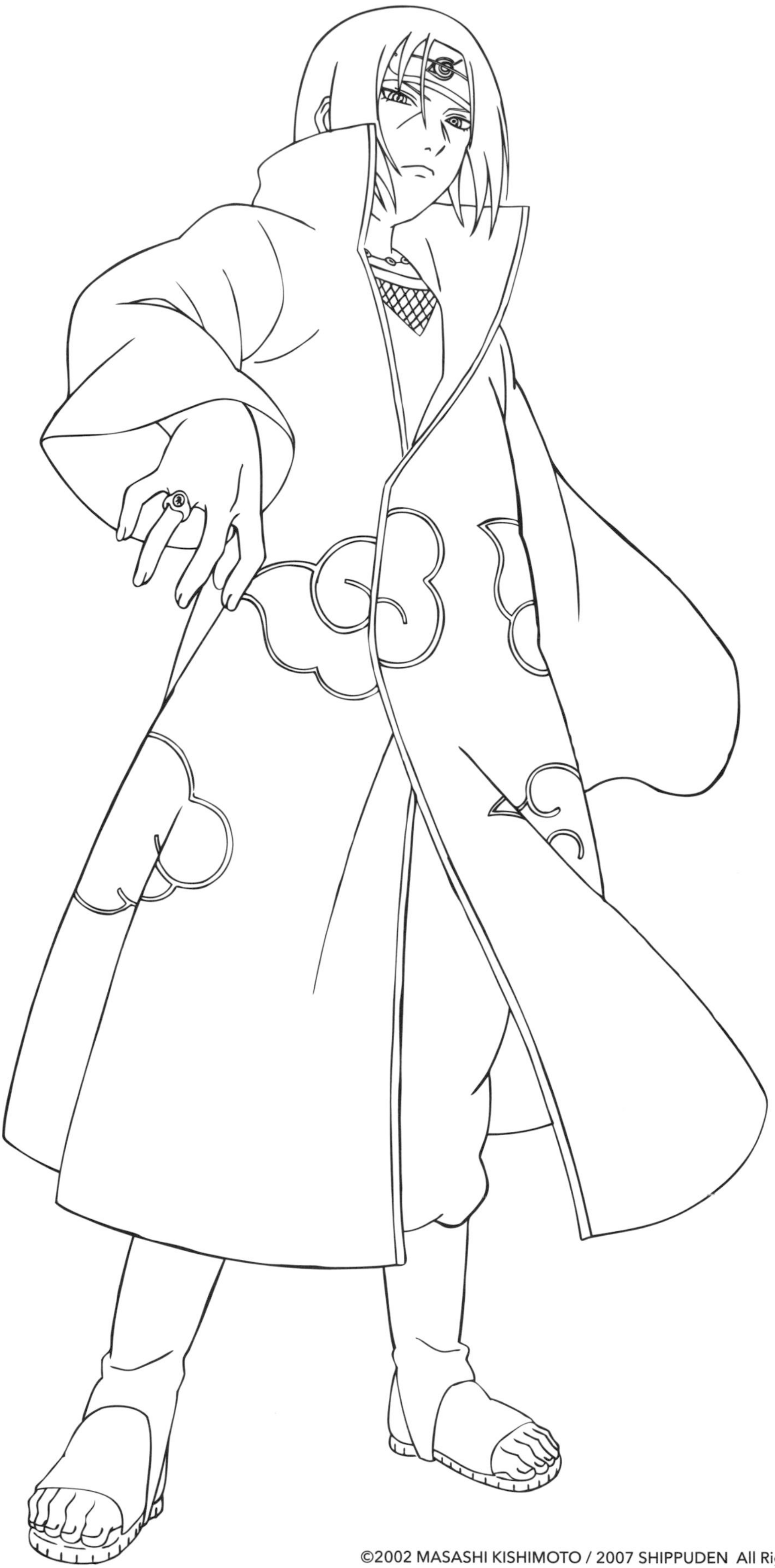

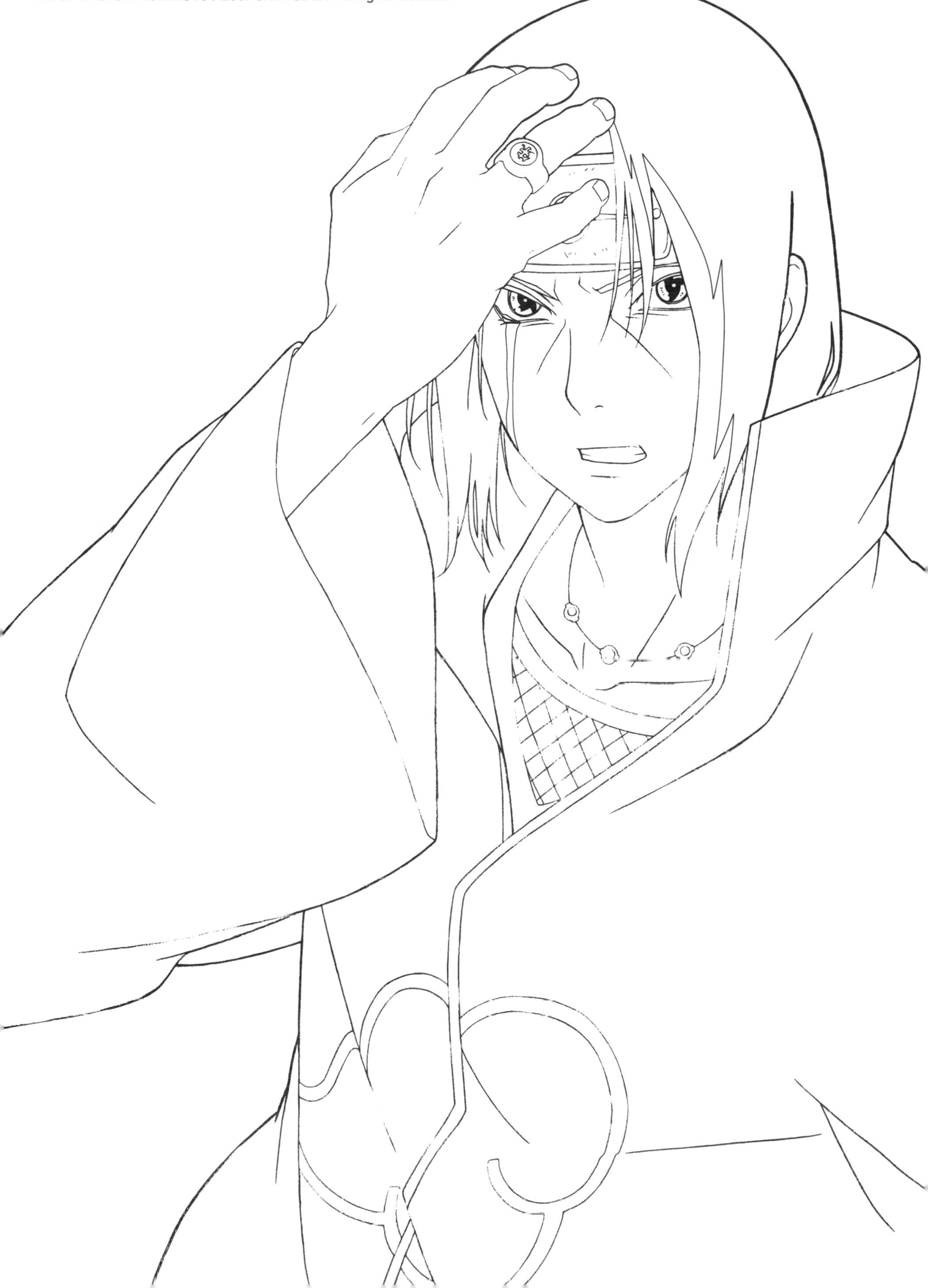

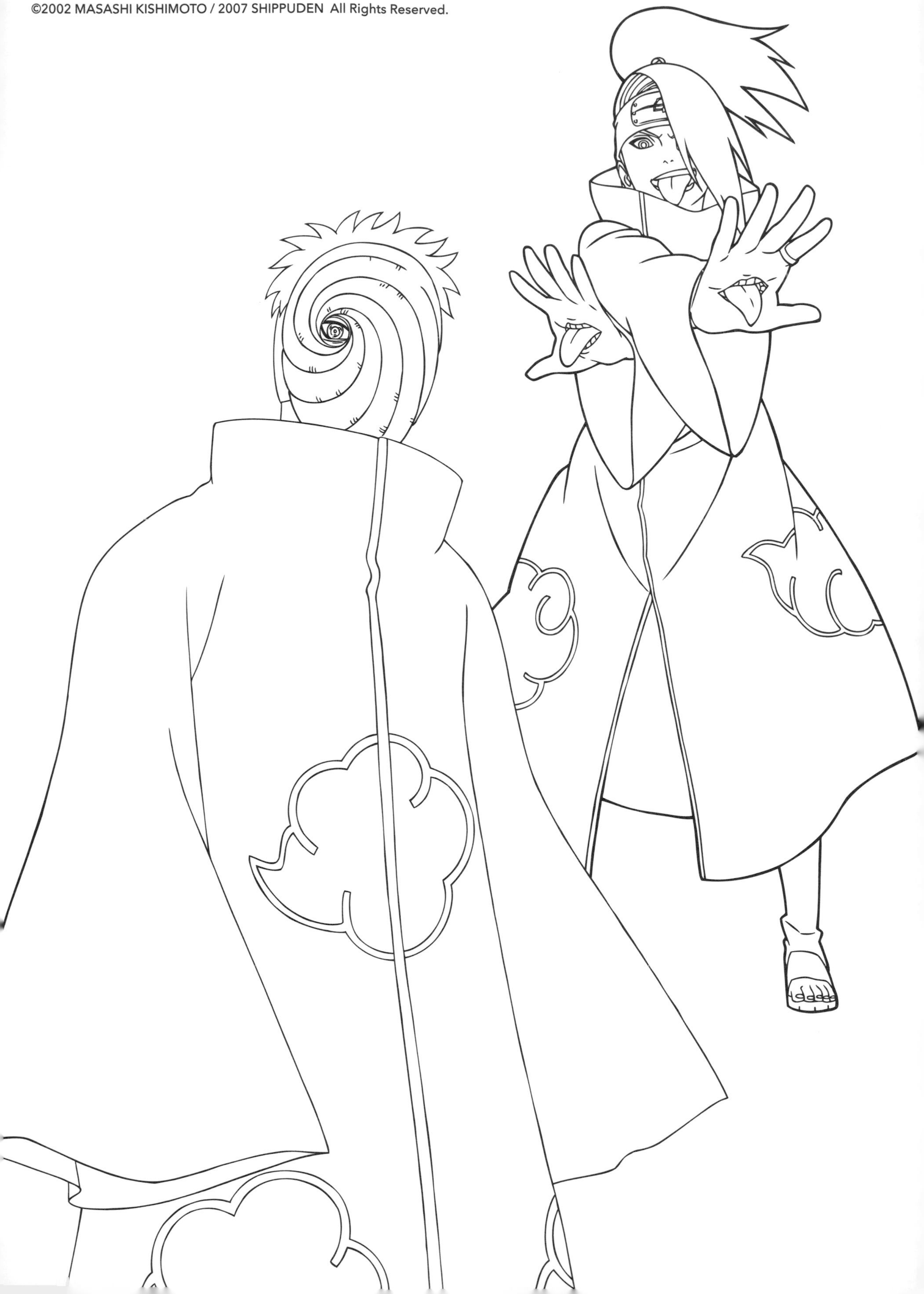

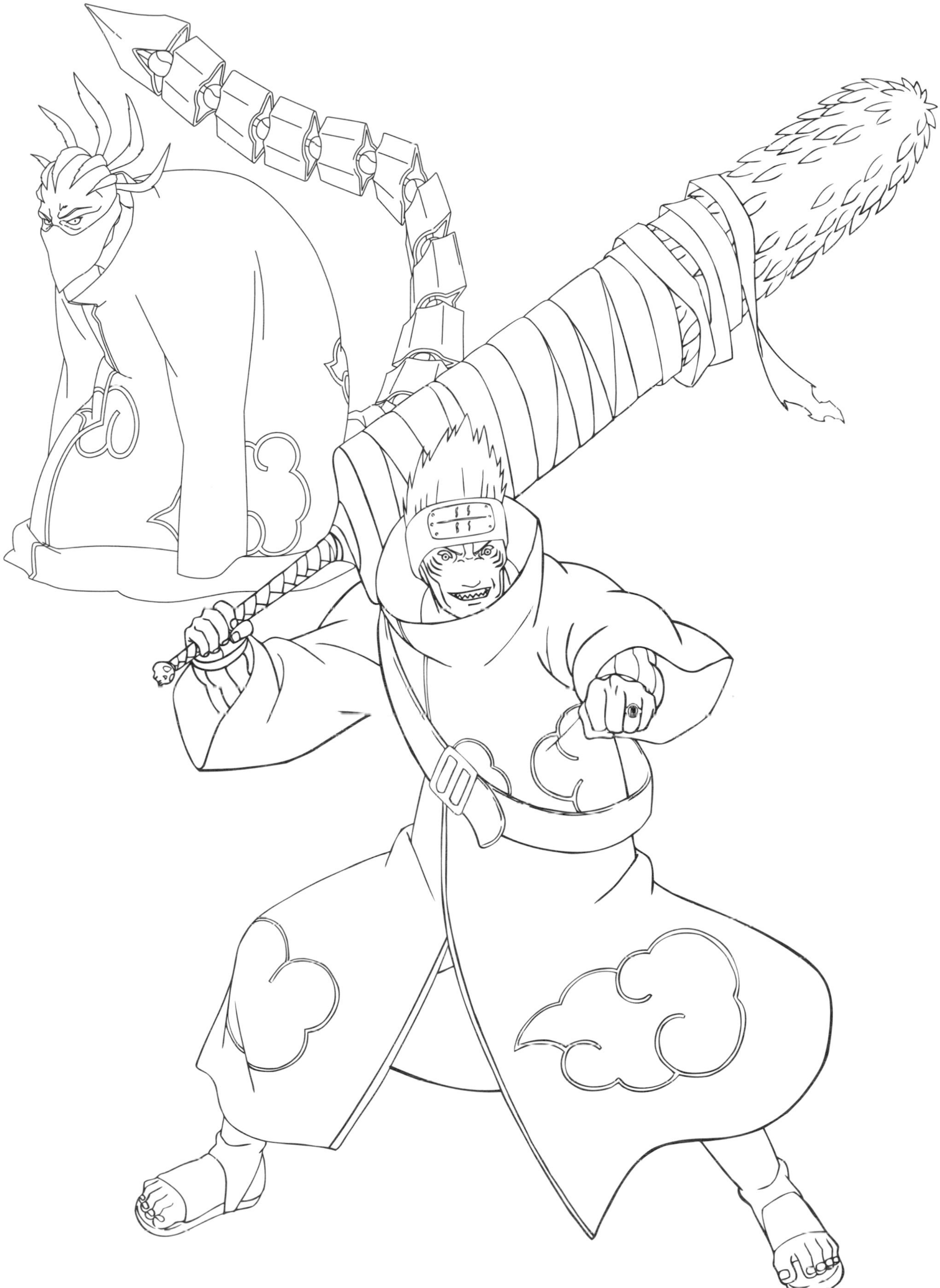

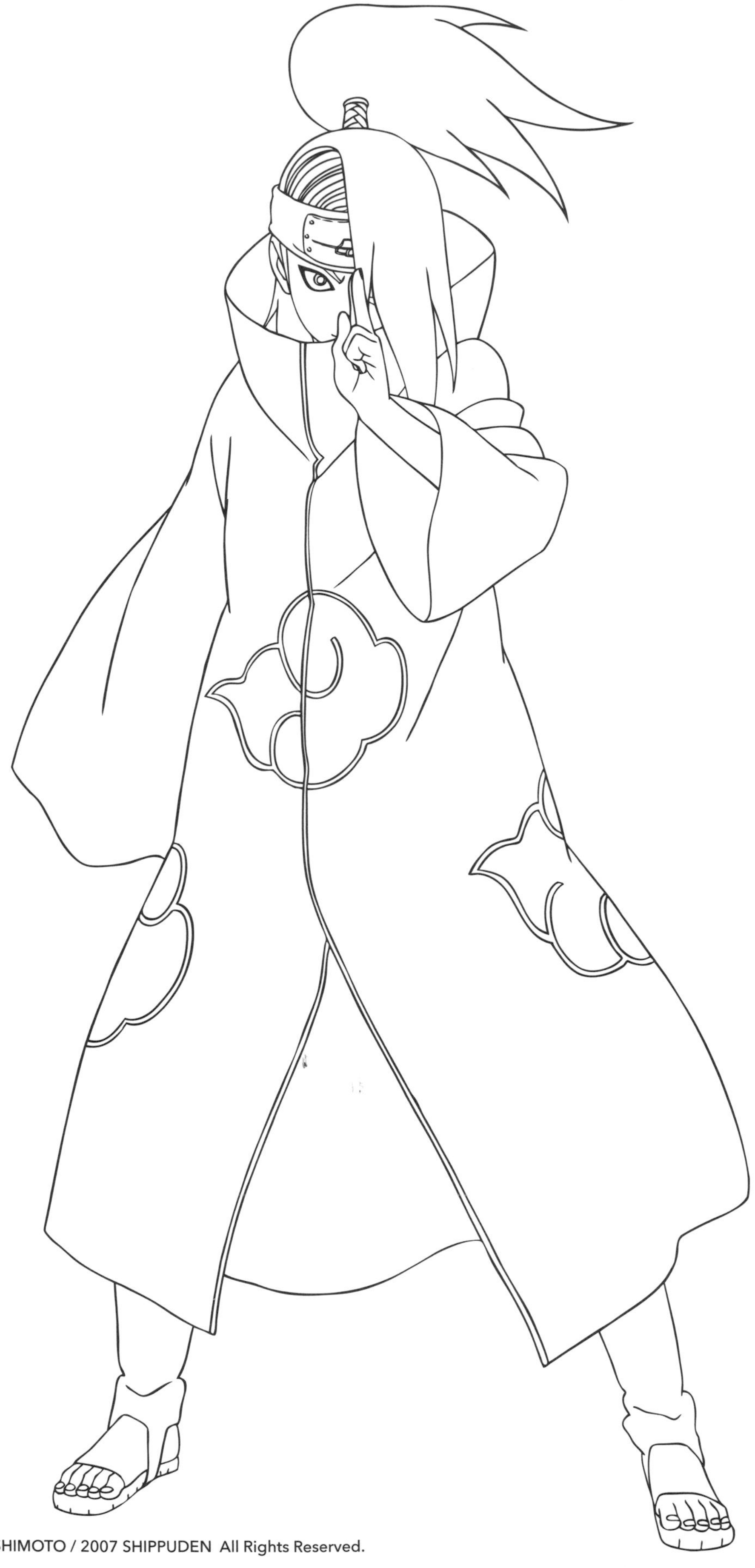

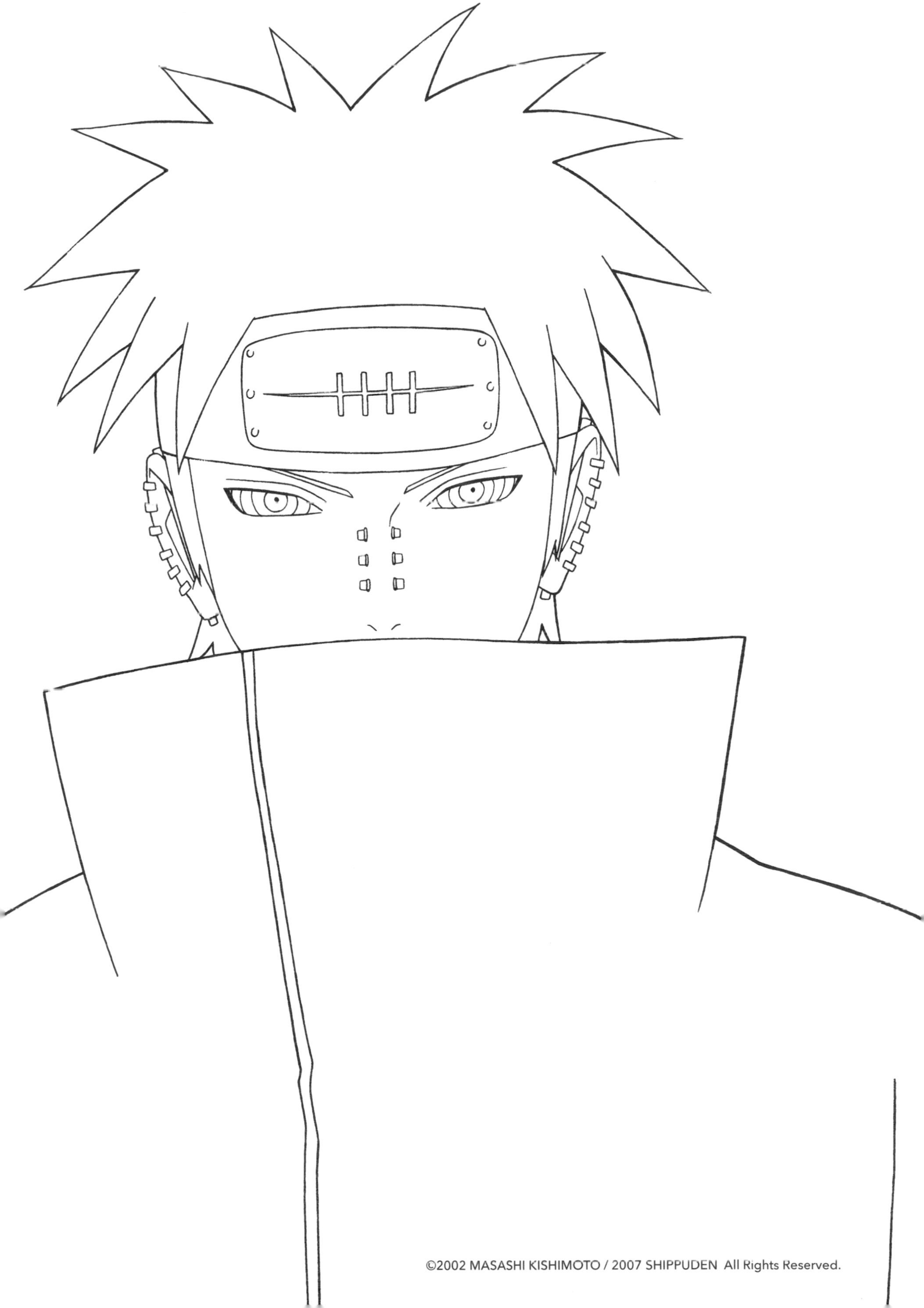

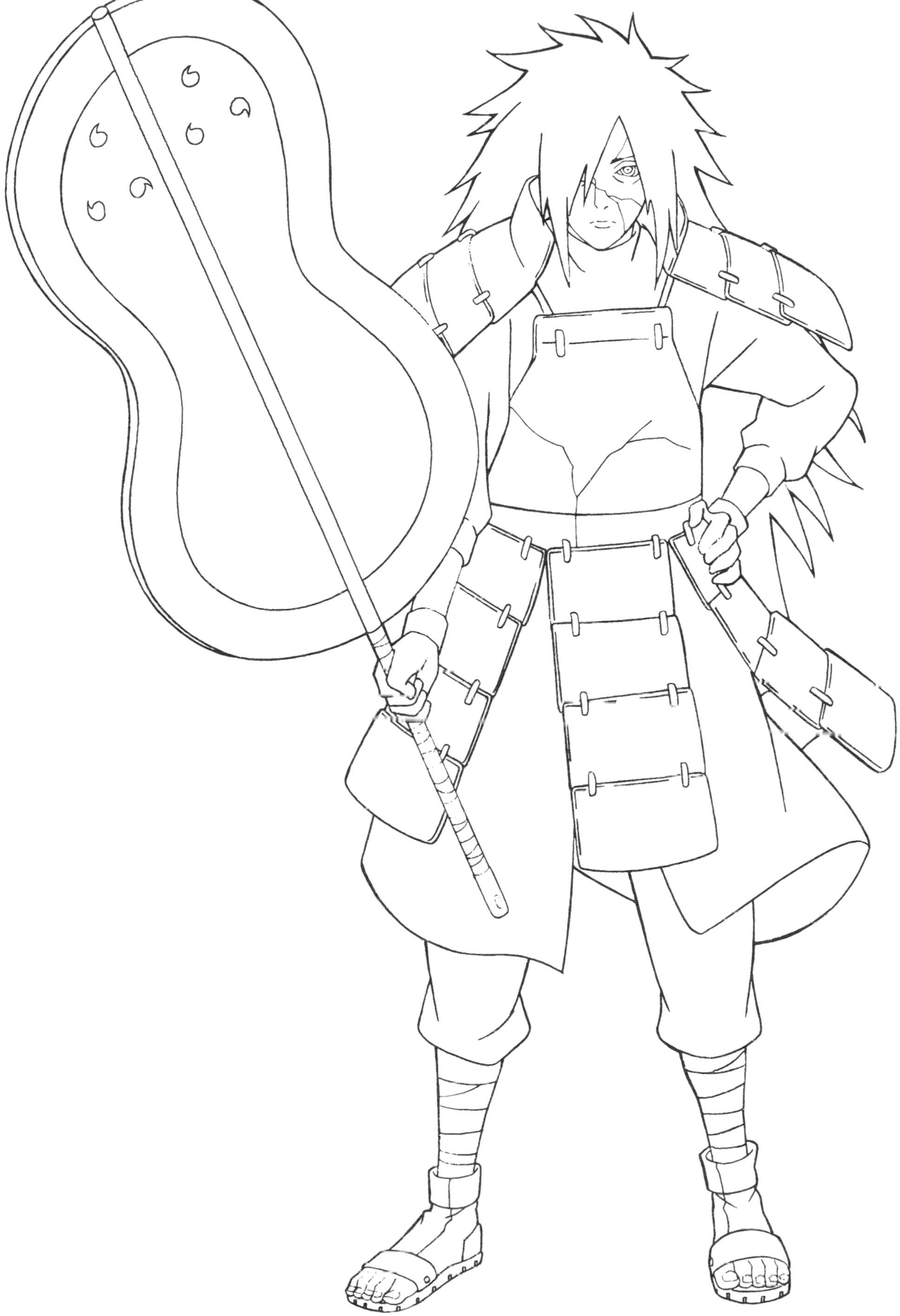

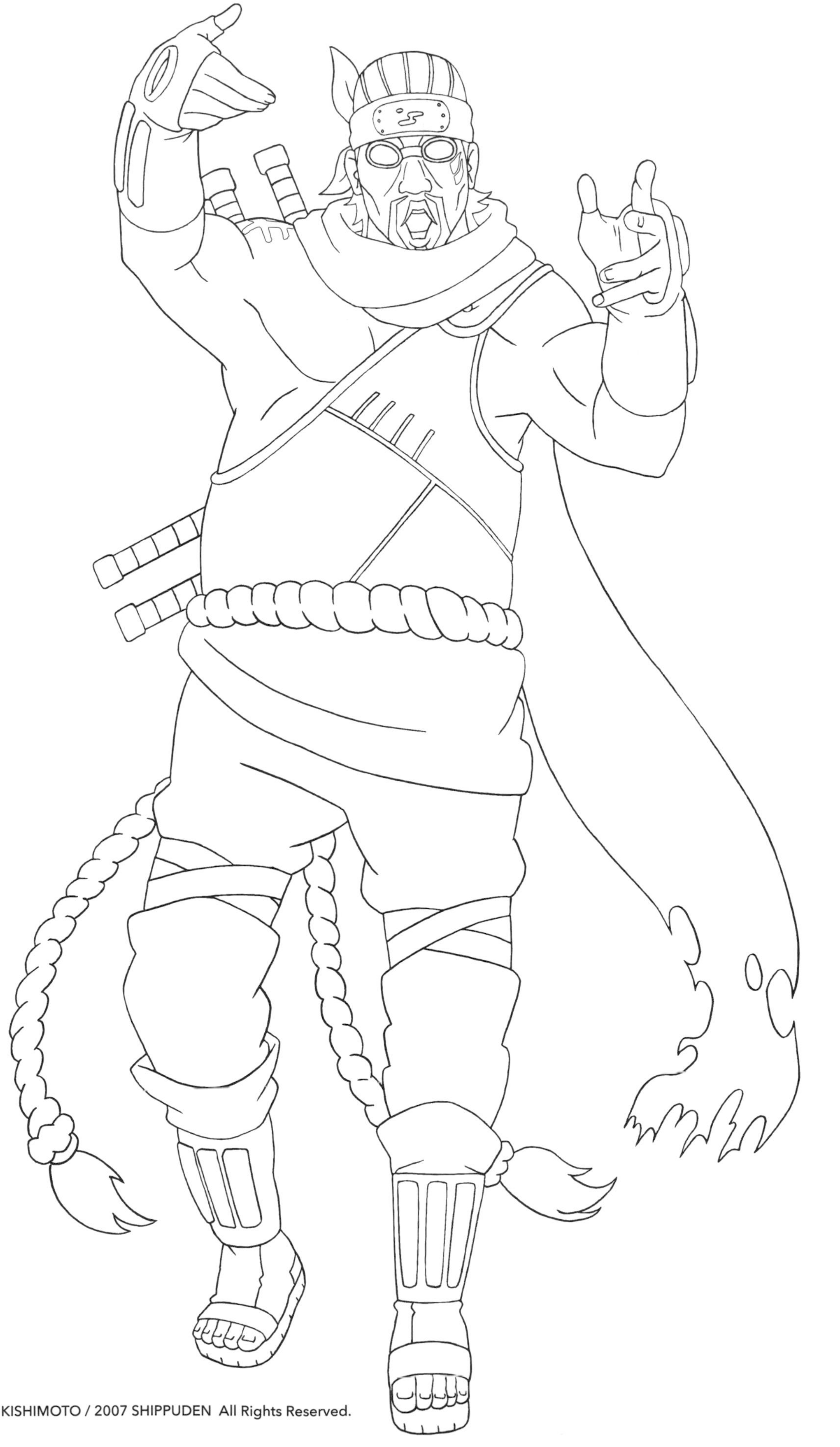

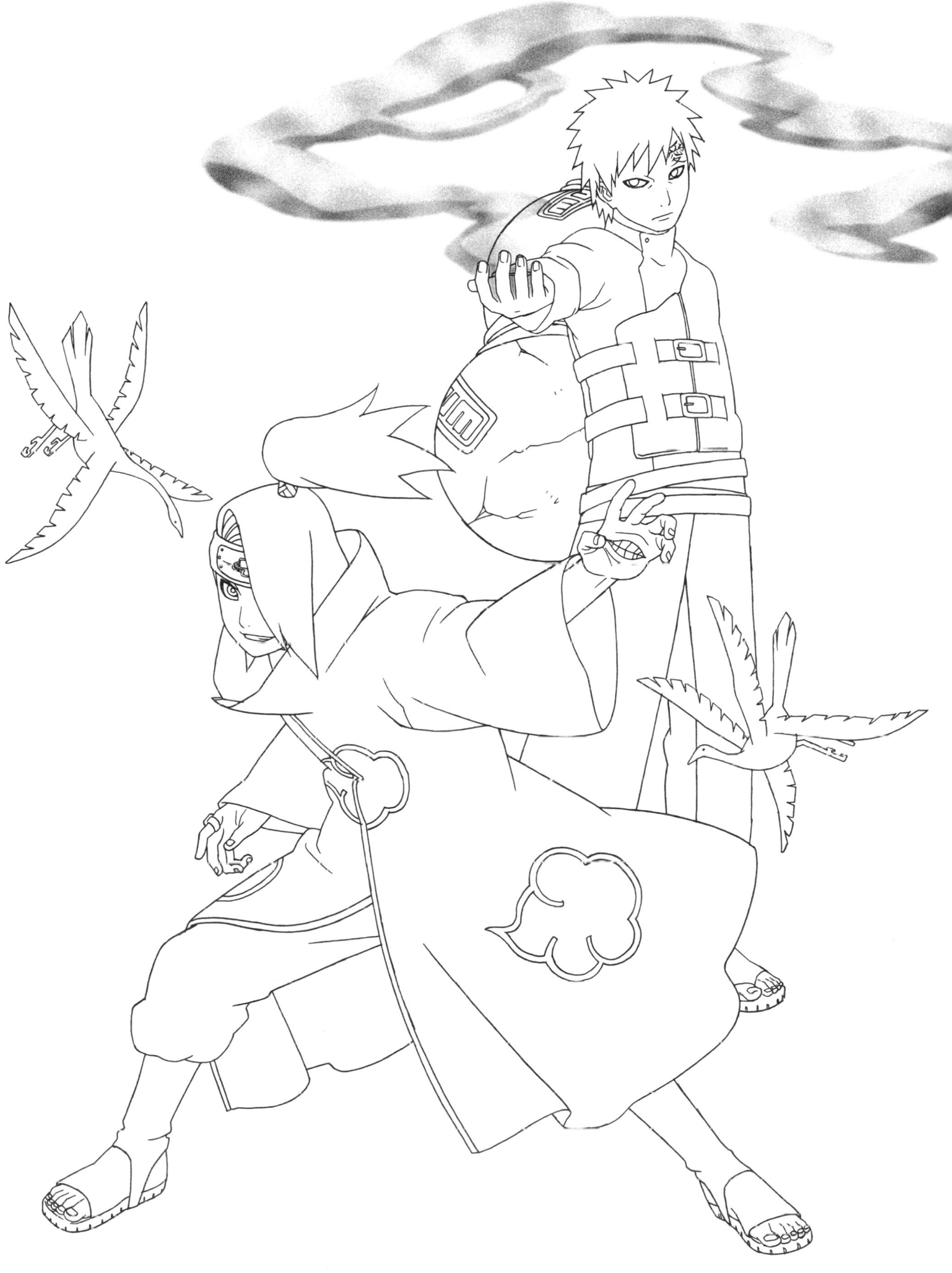

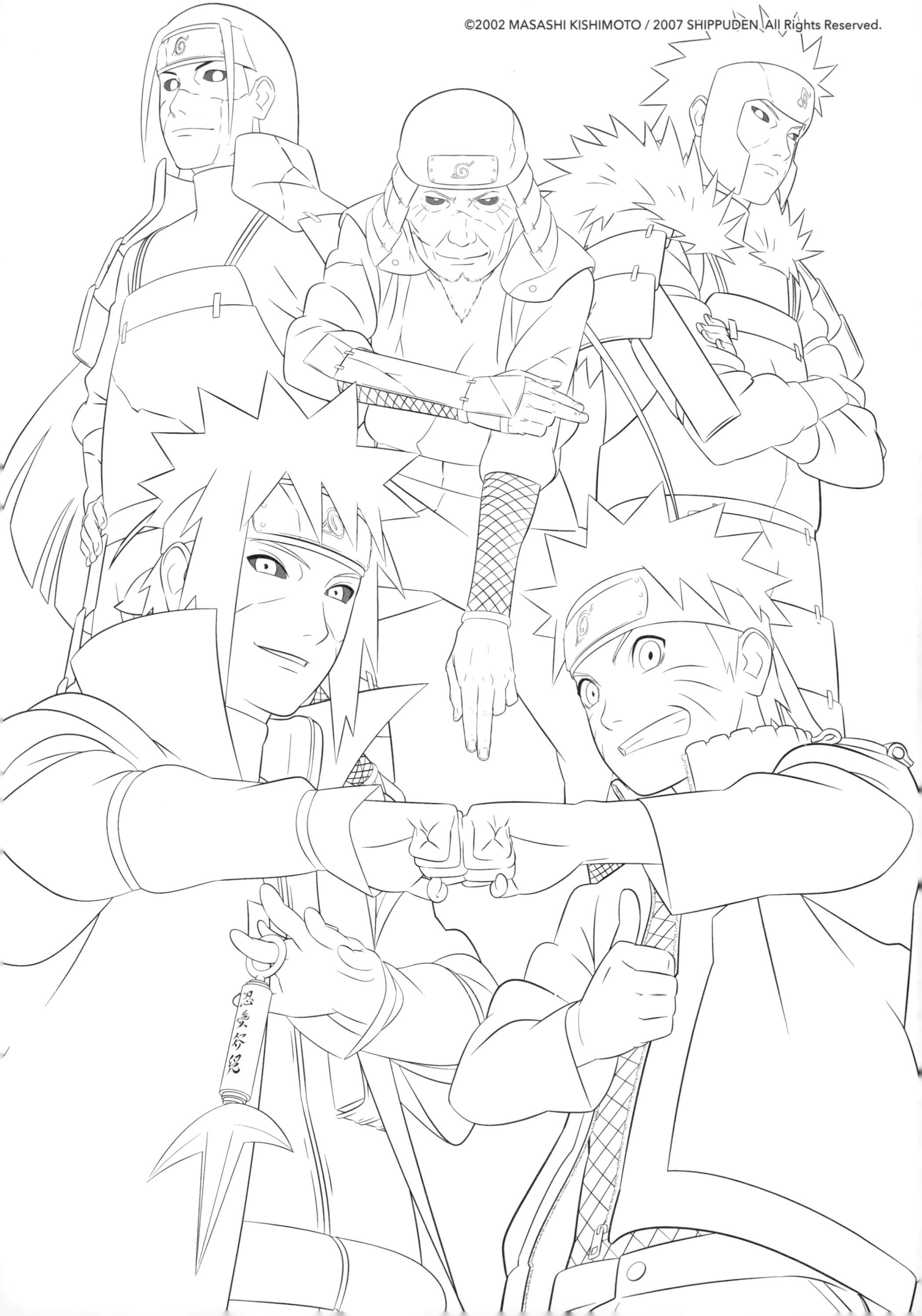